'At last we have an easy-to-read and engaging manual which provides parents with invaluable information on the sensory aspects of food as perceived by someone who has Asperger Syndrome. The text subsequently provides a rationale, framework and effective strategies to encourage a wider range of ingredients in meals. This book could transform the emotional atmosphere in the kitchen and dining room to the great relief of all family members.'

– *Tony Attwood, PhD, Clinical Psychologist, Minds & Hearts Clinic, Australia, and author of* The Complete Guide to Asperger's Syndrome

'Sarah Patten clearly understands food, and Asperger Syndrome! And this shines through as she describes her son's initially tentative, yet increasingly daring, relationship with food. Henry's journey with food is told with love, warmth and humour, and the mouth-watering recipes are sure to make you feel hungry, too!'

– *Jane Donlan, Co-Founder of ASK-PERGERS? and co-author of* Create a Reward Plan for your child with Asperger Syndrome *and* Helping Children with Autism Spectrum Conditions through Everyday Transitions

D0752407
...uth Services
Taunton Public Library

Youth Services
Taunton Public Library

What to Feed an Asperger

*How to go from
3 foods to 300 with love,
patience and a little sleight of hand*

Sarah Patten

Jessica Kingsley *Publishers*
London and Philadelphia

First published in 2015
by Jessica Kingsley Publishers
73 Collier Street
London N1 9BE, UK
and
400 Market Street, Suite 400
Philadelphia, PA 19106, USA

www.jkp.com

Copyright © Sarah Patten 2015

All rights reserved. No part of this publication may be reproduced in any material form (including photocopying or storing it in any medium by electronic means and whether or not transiently or incidentally to some other use of this publication) without the written permission of the copyright owner except in accordance with the provisions of the Copyright, Designs and Patents Act 1988 or under the terms of a licence issued by the Copyright Licensing Agency Ltd, Saffron House, 6–10 Kirby Street, London EC1N 8TS. Applications for the copyright owner's written permission to reproduce any part of this publication should be addressed to the publisher.

All pages marked ★ can be downloaded at www.jkp.com/catalogue/book/ 9781849057684/resources for personal use with this programme, but may not be reproduced for any other purposes without the permission of the publisher.

Warning: The doing of an unauthorized act in relation to a copyright work may result in both a civil claim for damages and criminal prosecution.

Library of Congress Cataloging in Publication Data
Patten, Sarah.
  What to feed an Asperger : how to go from three foods
to three hundred with love, patience and a
little sleight of hand / Sarah Patten.
    pages cm
  ISBN 978-1-84905-768-4 (alk. paper)
  1. Asperger's syndrome in children–Patients–Nutrition.
  2. Parents of autistic children. I. Title.
  RJ506.A9P35 2015
  618.92'858832–dc23
                                    2014024725

British Library Cataloguing in Publication Data
A CIP catalogue record for this book is available from the British Library

ISBN 978 1 84905 768 4
eISBN 978 0 85700 993 7

Printed and bound in Great Britain

MIX
Paper from
responsible sources
FSC
www.fsc.org   FSC® C013056

3 2872 50110 1103

To Dave, with love

Acknowledgements

Grateful thanks to Tatiana Miller, Victoria Peters and Deborah Barr, William Patten for his support and patience, and particularly my editor Rachel Menzies for her kind, incisive steerage. My most affectionate and deepest thanks are of course reserved for Henry, because without him my life would have been unimaginably poorer.

Contents

List of Recipes

Preface

A delicate and complex child with Asperger Syndrome requires a calm, unflappable parent, willing to take extra time out to nurture kindly and focus on their special needs. I am not that parent. Brusque and blunt by nature, I am the antithesis of an Asperger's parenting ideal. Maybe that's why, immersed in my own work and busy schedule, I failed for so many years to tune in to who Henry really was. Though, *je ne regrette rien*, as they say.

But I like to think that the clash of my action-oriented personality and Henry's introverted, thoughtful self, aged seven, created sufficient friction to bring things to a head. The ever-diminishing list on Henry's menu, indeed his whole approach to food, was driving me crazy. My insistence that he just eat what was put in front of him caused Henry obvious mental anguish and he pushed back with increasing anger and frustration. So we hit that tipping point and then got on track to fix it.

This is a journey I want to relate because all our lives have been improved by making a few simple changes. We now have happy family mealtimes and I feel connected to a child who four years ago was a difficult stranger. There must be a whole bunch of you out there who can benefit from the route we've taken and the discoveries we've made, whether you embrace it wholesale or cherry-pick the bits that fit best for you. Not only has this upgraded diet dramatically enhanced Henry's ability to focus and function, it has entirely reset his eating habits. I now have a balanced, happy, even-tempered child able to hold his own at a regular high school. He has a bright future. This surely is a story worth sharing.

Introduction

What's the Problem?

This parenting cookbook is packed full
of mealtime tips and tricks to improve
the diet of super-sensitive Asperger kids.

I am the mother of an 11-year-old boy
with Asperger's. Four years ago I had a child
whose limited diet and refusal to eat all but three
foods was causing both of us deep distress. Family mealtimes
were pure hell: 'Come on now, Henry, eat the sausage! It's a
sausage! How hard can it be?' Followed by hysterics from Henry
who didn't then have the vocabulary to explain that skins on
sausages were repellent. Furthermore, the herby bits in them
pretty much sent him over the edge.

It is easy to dismiss faddy behaviour as just another phase.
I am guilty of putting Henry's increasingly bizarre eating habits
down to the 'terrible twos', which then rolled on year by year,
ending with the 'psychotic sixes'. And I still thought that at some
point Henry would emerge the other side of whatever this was
and eat normally. Denial! Just looking at the way his brother ate
compared with Henry should have been enough of a wake-up
call. Will, aged five, would be happily chowing down on Pad Thai
noodles with shrimp, egg, bean sprouts, soy sauce – the whole
shooting match. Across the table Henry had a plate of plain
noodles that he eyed with extreme caution, accompanied by the
obligatory piece of chicken on a separate plate, complaining that
the spicy smells from Will's food were upsetting his calm.

Bizarrely, Henry enjoyed a full and varied diet up to the age of about two, and then someone flicked a switch and only chicken, bread and dry cereal were on the menu. If it wasn't bland and white, he wouldn't touch it. Added to that, the elements of his meal had to be served on separate plates. Any suggestion from me that he tried, say, a nice bit of beef stew was met with serious anxiety that worked up to hysterics. So eating beyond the three white 'safe' foods was a problem, foods touching was a problem, even odours from our food was a problem, and all this usually ended in Henry leaving the table an unhappy, sad boy, having only eaten a mouthful of chicken or bread. This was distressing and horrible for Henry and everyone around him.

At this stage he hadn't been diagnosed (I hate that term because I don't think he's ill) and the only advice I was given from the medical profession was that most children his age were picky eaters and I had to be patient. Patience didn't work. Neither did bribery, coaxing, cajoling, reasoning or ordering. And, I am ashamed to say, threatening. None of it worked. Things just got worse.

I reached a point at which Henry's behaviour couldn't be explained away any more by his age, a bad day at school or any other excuse. I hated what mealtimes had become and it saddened me that I had a child who couldn't enjoy his food and, what's more, was missing vital nutrients in his limited diet. He was already very thin, with dark rings under his eyes. I no longer believed that he was 'just being awkward' or belligerent to get his own way. This situation was out of control and something had to be done.

So I decided to take a good hard look at my lovely boy and really try to understand food from his angle. We had a long weepy chat during which he told me that food didn't feel nice in his mouth. The way he described how disgusting and unpleasant a piece of meat in sauce tastes, you would think I had forced him to eat slugs or rats' droppings. How could a nice homemade beef stew evoke that level of repulsion? (I know you are thinking it and my beef stews are pretty good, by the way.) It seems that most textures, smells and tastes have an unbearable intensity. 'Too-strong tastes hurt my mouth,' he said. Garden peas, according to Henry, have that 'disgusting' combination of slimy exterior and pulpy interior, which makes them one of the worst things I can serve, apart from perhaps baked beans that have all the revolting pea characteristics but in a 'slippy' sauce. Horror of horrors! I soon realized this wasn't Henry's problem but *my* problem. I hadn't tuned in to a fundamental feature of my son's make-up. I felt I was failing him and I wanted to make it right.

I now know that an Asperger's nervous system works rather differently to ours. The human brain continually processes information received from receptors all over our body, helping us organize, prioritize and understand the world around us. Chemical receptors on our tongue are capable of relaying a myriad of messages about what we have in our mouths. Whether it is salty, sour, sweet, its temperature and texture. For an Asperger these receptors are either turned down and are *hypo*sensitive, or cranked right up to maximum and are *hyper*sensitive. Hypo kids love extremely spicy and strong-tasting foods and continually crave intense flavours, even to the point of trying non-foods to get that taste satisfaction. In this book, though, I will concentrate on our own experience of hypersensitivity and the job we've had combatting Henry's screening and oral defensiveness.

What I want to say very loud and clear to all those mums, dads and carers of Aspies out there is that YOU ARE NOT ALONE in your struggle. And that it is not OK when a well-meaning friend or relative says, 'Just as long as he's eating *something*, that's fine.' It isn't. Or, 'Most kids are faddy eaters; he'll grow out of it.' He won't. All children need nutrients today – right now, not later. Get inside your kid's head and learn how they experience food and then work with it. Here's how.

Chapter 1

Knowing Me, Knowing You
(There is Something We Can Do)

We needed to get to the bottom of exactly what worked and didn't work food-wise on Henry's sensory map, and why. Over several sessions we laid out fruit, vegetables and various family meals on the kitchen counter and discussed their merits and demerits. We drew them and pulled them apart, and I encouraged Henry to share as much about how he experienced these foods as possible. We started this journey of exploration by getting to grips with the foods central to Henry's diet at age seven. What was so special about chicken breast meat, bread and dry cereal? My first mistake had been to  assume it was all about taste and texture, because Henry started out by critiquing each of these favourites at great length based purely on appearance. All were, of course, uniformly white or cream-coloured, free from dubious 'bits' such as herbs or seeds that could be seen. He also focused on the uniformity of their shape. The regularity of the cereal Os and squares pleased him, and a chicken breast takes on pretty much the same form from meal to meal. He preferred bread with the crusts cut off, but such was his all-consuming (!) love of bread that he would accept it in almost any shape and size. This, incidentally, gave me an idea of how to move forward because any food presented as bread would be happily eaten. But more on that later.

With chicken, bread and cereal, what you see is what you get. There are no hidden cavities holding mixed-textured elements such as watery stuff or seeds, no hard bits like nuts to take you by surprise. They look bland and have a characteristic shape, and that security is extended through to their taste and texture. Nothing challenging in either department.

The fun started when we embarked on a grand appraisal of a selection of foods I knew gave him the screaming heebie-jeebies, and again we tried to get to the bottom of why. Henry studied an assortment of edibles laid out before him and I was at pains to make clear that he was required to touch and inspect but wouldn't be made to eat them; what I wanted was as much information as possible without upsetting him with the prospect of having to put these repugnant foods into his mouth.

As expected, foods that deviated furthest away from the adored white, bland and even texture were most reviled. In other words, anything brightly coloured, multi-textured and spicy. Oranges tick all three of these boxes – in this case, exchanging spicy for acidic because in Henry's mind they amount to the same. He would only entertain exploring the central fleshy part of an orange segment as the combination of the skin encasing the segments and the white fibrous strands was entirely too challenging and revolting. With only the briefest sniff, he recoiled and described what he knew would be a harsh, unpleasant assault on his taste buds. It was a reaction that I might have at the prospect of biting into a lemon or a strong onion. This was all good information and tuned me in to the idea that his taste buds were working on overdrive and that, in comparison, mine were dulled and hard-of-tasting.

On to the meats, fish and other sources of protein. I would have loved to have had cheese in Henry's diet at this stage because it's such great source of protein and calcium, but he found even the mildest Cheddar intolerable. Henry had had a particularly bad bout of gastroenteritis at 18 months which rendered him lactose intolerant, and so he may connect cheese with stomach aches. We tried him with goat's milk and that didn't make him sick. He definitely acquired a taste for it because he drank pints and pints of it until, at the age of six, he was able to switch back to cow's milk, but he never made it to cheese. So I am not sure that theory holds water (or milk). The fact remains, though, that cheese was a sticking point; try as I may, I couldn't get him to go near it, let alone describe what it was about it that he found so abhorrent. Nuts were also unspeakably horrible and that's as far as that went. I had more luck with fish and meat. When I presented a thick slice of lamb to him, on initial inspection he thought it was chicken and, rightly or wrongly, I didn't correct him. I was very keen to get fish into his diet. And I mean *real* fish, not the finger or breadcrumbed variety. We did fish quite thoroughly and found that very fresh non-fishy-smelling fish with a mild flavour would not be refused outright, especially if it was presented as a shape that resembled a chicken breast. This sounds a bit far-fetched, I know, but white fish fried in the same way as I would fry a piece of chicken didn't evoke that initial visual rejection. This was a very important discovery. Get past that visual screening by presenting a new food to look like a favoured one and that food had a much higher chance of being eaten.

Next we moved on to sauces and gravies. Butter and spreads came into this category too. In essence, according to Henry, any food was rendered ten times more revolting by the presence of a sauce or spread. The very worst texture known to man or boy was 'slippy' and slimy, and Henry just couldn't understand why we ate it. Why, for instance, did we prefer a perfectly nice chicken breast covered with a cream sauce to having it 'just plain'? He got quite heated about this, as if the world was deliberately bent on sabotaging perfectly good food.

I wanted to get to the bottom of the sauce/spread issue, but apparently the sensation was too awful for words and all I got by way of an explanation was gagging and choking noises, coupled with a great deal of shuddering and shaking of hands. Despite this minor setback, we persisted with the information gathering because I felt that if I could figure out a feature of his most hated foods that I could fix, then we would have a starting point from which to move forward.

So we continued in our quest and ploughed through acres of fruit and vegetables as they were top of my list to incorporate into his diet. I stripped the fresh produce aisles at Whole Foods (from Henry being aged two to nine we lived near Chicago before moving back to Tunbridge Wells) and created a fruit-and-veggie smorgasbord, and Henry in turn addressed their pros (hardly any) and cons (everything) as we went along. From this extensive discussion we sectioned fruits and vegetables into three categories based on their potential as possible foods for Henry. And here they are:

1. Absolutely no way; would cross the street to avoid

Tomatoes: plastic coated with disgusting slippy pips, watery sauce and harsh acid taste. Worst kind: cherry tomatoes that explode all of the above into your mouth.

Broad beans, cucumber, blueberries, grapes, peppers, eggplant/aubergines and peas, to name a few, share that same tomato characteristic of a smooth, tight skin with a challenging interior, sometimes hiding 'gritty' seeds.

Chillis, olives, radish, pineapple, kiwi and mango have a smell and flavour so overpowering as to be utterly repulsive. Now, I can understand that for chillis, olives and radish, because how many children (with the exception of Henry's brother) do like these? But *mango*? Mangos are gorgeous – that is, if they have been allowed to ripen and not shoved into cold storage too early. But no, mangos are too strong and not to be tolerated.

Mushrooms, raspberries, celery, sugar-snap peas, corn (on and off the cob), fennel, celeriac, French beans, avocado, blackberries, strawberries and a whole host of others have horrible textures, either single or multiple. Leeks, for instance, 'squeak'.

2. Less hateful

Peeled potatoes (with every dark bit cut off), bananas, lettuce and mild salad leaves, parsnips, cabbage, peeled pears, swede and squash, sweet potato, seedless mild melon such as galia and honeydew, peeled baby zucchini/courgettes (seedless) and, surprisingly, asparagus are all less offensive than the above list. Texture is a large consideration, and they are all quite mild in flavour and either green or pale in colour. Even a banana, peeled, becomes an acceptable creamy colour.

3. Some redeeming features

Peeled and cored apples, peeled young carrots, fine green beans, broccoli and kale were all interesting in some way or other and, with the exception of the carrots, were green, which was the most tolerated colour for food after white or cream. I had a feeling that, diet-wise, green was becoming the new cream.

Connections

The structure of broccoli really caught Henry's attention and he loved the infinitesimal branching. There's no doubt that Henry is a scientist by nature. From being a small child he's always had a perceptive, enquiring mind and engaged deeply with an object, seeing abstract features that, quite frankly, passed me by. He's studied everything around him, from the structure of his layered cereal squares to the vacuum cleaner, and made quite startling observations on their engineering and function. On walks he's been known to stop by a plant, say a foxglove, and assess it for 20 minutes, fully appreciating the shape and pattern in extreme detail. So this recognition of structure and form came into play when we were looking at the food, and I hoped we could use it to change Henry's attitude towards fruit and vegetables, and get him to see them on more friendly terms, even if it was because they had a Fibonacci branching sequence. Suddenly, broccoli was no longer an unpleasant foreign food but a mathematical model and a template with which to compare other plants. Brussels sprouts on the stem, lettuce and cabbage leaves arranged around the stalk all follow a set pattern and ratio of division. So science and mathematics gave us our 'in' with vegetables. On this particular track there's a lot to get into. Have you noticed how curly kale leaves expand as they furl out, and how the curves and twists towards the end in turn create a surface area that just seems to get bigger and bigger? It's what mathematicians call a hyperbolic form. Henry loves it, and it gave him a new, exciting relationship to his food.

I don't expect that maths or science is everyone's thing, but it really has made a huge difference to us because there's now something pleasant and interesting about these veggies that somehow makes them more attractive to have around. Mothers of neurotypical children for ever have been making vegetables on a plate into smiley faces or using train noises to get food into the 'tunnel'. But for Aspergers who view their world in quite a different way, I think a more in-depth approach is needed. So find out what floats your kid's boat. Are they into shapes or patterns? Do they like conformity? We know Aspies who are devoted *Star Trek* nuts. What do those Trekkies eat come lunchtime on the Starship Enterprise? Do whatever it takes to get past that initial knee-jerk reaction that instantly rejects food that doesn't fit their limited criteria.

Making a start

Pick a new food and go for it. We chose broccoli, and I started by introducing the smallest floret on a separate plate every day and asking Henry, in a very matter-of-fact way, to eat it. We didn't discuss its mathematical merits at the table, as that had all been part of gaining its acceptance. Now it was food to be viewed only as food and it was on his plate at lunch or dinnertime every day. I know every day does sound intense. Who wants to eat the same food every day? Well, an Asperger does. They love familiar, they love routine. The first few times Henry ate the broccoli he made a fuss, but actually not a huge fuss. I, in turn, showed no emotion about the thing. As far as I was concerned, here we all were eating broccoli and that was *absolutely normal*. And do you know, after the second week, it really was. Pretty soon, heaps of broccoli were being consumed every day, raw or lightly steamed. He was the only kid at school with raw broccoli in his lunch box. Even now, Henry eats this green floral stuff at least three times a week; it has just become another routine and he has completely accepted its presence on his plate. I know that when your child eats his or her first proper serving of vegetables, it will be as big a deal for you as it was for me. It's a start, a very small start, but now, with a plan and stacks of determination, you know there is a way forward and so you keep going.

Key foods and a rough time frame

We aimed for one new food a week. Broccoli actually was a breeze, but for some foods a weekly introduction was a bit ambitious and we definitely dragged our feet a little bit if our current food was proving to be more of a challenge (I remember bananas taking a while). Based on the food critiquing conversations Henry and I had had, we agreed on a 'foods to try list' and our first one went something like this: fruit (apples, pears, bananas), vegetables (broccoli, carrots and beans), fish, eggs and brown rice. And right there I had vitamins, protein, omegas, calcium and calming Bs parcelled in a beautiful, complex, slow-burning carbohydrate. It was very much a 'Let's try these because we know they have potential' rather than a 'You will try them and like them' approach. And since we had discussed their good points at length, they had already passed an initial screening. To help things along, Henry seemed to appreciate that I 'got it' in terms of why some foods were potential winners and why others would never be entertained. So stay positive about this plan and leave out any emotion along the lines of 'Will he like it or won't he like it?' For my child a matter-of-fact, moving-forward approach worked. All previous fervent cajoling and persuading had been exactly the wrong mindset. And now we had 'This is our plan, it's a great plan and we're doing it.'

From broccoli and apple we worked up to fish. After some consideration I plumped for coley, which is the preferred white, about as mild a tasting fish as you can get, and actually, if you care, a sustainable substitute for our disappearing cod. I did manage to get Henry to eat salmon, but much later when he was about nine and only the farmed variety, which has a milder flavour and is paler in colour. Unbelievably, brown rice was a great success and pretty much replaced bread for a while. Henry ate brown rice every day for two years! Carrots were as easy as broccoli and, like broccoli, had to be eaten raw or at least crunchy. Then we hit a sticking point because, as far as Henry was concerned, broccoli and carrots were really the only veg worth eating, so I am afraid I stooped to sibling competition to get him to eat green beans (sometimes called French beans). First we guessed the 'number of the bean' – that is, how many counts it will take to eat the bean. It has to be crunched on entering the mouth, by the way, and not bent in whole. That's cheating. So green-bean-eating competitions with his brother worked well until they tired of that game and started smoking them instead, which I tried to discourage, although it was very funny.

Trying new foods is difficult and stressful for your child. Never lose sight of that. Keep to your plan but, along the way, tune in to your Asperger's emotional state. I was so encouraged by our initial success that I powered forward, riding a bit roughshod over Henry's delicate sensibilities, and that set us back a bit. So take a quick 'temperature check' and ensure your child is calm and happy before throwing a new dietary challenge at them. If all's not well and it's lunchtime, try it at dinnertime instead. Just don't choose the day the dog has chewed his favourite Lego® mini-figure as the day to introduce eggplant/aubergines.

Just the smallest, teeniest bite

The biggest hurdle, of course, is getting your child to try the food in the first place and then eat it again and again until it is accepted without any fuss. Perhaps you will have found out that there's nothing about that particular food that they absolutely refuse to tolerate, and maybe you'll have previously made a connection with it – something that piques their interest. Start out by presenting the tiniest bit of it and asking your child to eat it. Note here that I don't ask that they *try* it, but that they *eat* it. Rejection should not be offered as an option. The bite should be so small and insignificant that it shouldn't look too intimidating. Even if they squirm and hate it, treat this event as if it's nothing out of the ordinary and give them glowing but not exuberant praise. The next day offer the same tiny piece and the same routine and just keep going.

If you really hit a sticking point with a new food and they won't try it or it is causing genuine distress, try presenting the food in a different form. Apples disliked raw might be tolerated pureed. We had great success with corn: on the cob or as nibbits it was detested, but it was happily consumed when creamed. Ditto for spinach.

It is really important that they eat a bit of the new food regularly. I promise you that after a while they will just eat it without the prompting. It's about breaking old habits and establishing new ones.

Sleight of hand

The food introduction process was going well but at a snail's pace and I wasn't sure, given his rate of growth, that this process was going to adequately meet Henry's protein and vitamin needs. Since bread was still his favourite food, I decided to rework this preferred staple and give it a nutrient boost. (See later chapters for fortified breads and cakes.) I found that if it looked white and bread-like, and didn't taste too dissimilar to his beloved farmhouse loaf or pitta, he would happily eat a bready or cake substitute made with quinoa flour, ground almonds and extra eggs to add protein, or cream, Greek yoghurt or crème fraîche to massively up the calcium.

Here's another tactic I use to fly under the radar and evade the visual screening that has Henry rejecting unfamiliar food before it actually hits his taste buds. It's easy; I just have the new food mimic what he knows and loves. So to get Henry eating lamb, I fried it slowly until super-tender and presented it to look just like a chicken breast. This worked with most meats. If something looks similar, call it by the same name.

And sometimes, when I am all out of inventive ways to serve up a new food, I have to just blag it.

'What is it, Mum?' Henry would say, quizzically eyeing the slice of fruit I had just handed him.

'It's a kind of apple. Nicer than the regular sort.'

'What's this kind of apple called?'

'It's a pear-apple. Really good.'

'Mummmm!'

'Try it, Henry, and then we'll talk about what you want to do for your birthday.'

I think because I am straight, honest and un-devious in every other area of Henry's life, he accepts that I use this unprincipled method to coerce him into trying new foods. If my duplicity upset him or undermined our relationship in any way, then I would desist. But thankfully he's very good-humoured about it.

I also disguise particularly wonderful nutrient-rich foods that I know are a long way off being accepted on their own. I make chocolate mousse with avocado, milkshakes with whey cheese, and cakes with challenging vegetables!

Exposure and familiarity is key

The challenging foods identified by chatting to your child don't have to be dismissed altogether. Most of the foods that Henry finds abhorrent – those being bright, flavourful and multi-textured ones, such as peppers, chillis, bean  stews and hot curries – are at the top of my husband's and younger son's list. And so, come mealtimes, who am I to please? As a solution, we have embraced buffet-style meals with a selection of dishes to cater for the full spectrum of our family's needs.

This meal plan serves two purposes: first, everyone gets to eat what they like; second, Henry is exposed to the colours and aromas that he finds offensive. Over time, familiarity with these bright pungent foods has made them more acceptable. He's not yet into chillis, but aged ten he did accept cheese and now grated cheese is freely sprinkled on his pizzas and in his fajitas.

Environmental issues

As we got deeper into this voyage of discovery, I began to realize that getting Henry to eat well wasn't all about the food and that how he felt within himself and what was happening around him played an important role in his food choices.

To see these patterns of behaviour more clearly, I made a diary over the period of a week. You might also find this exercise useful (a template for this 'Food and Mood Diary' is included in the Appendix and can be downloaded from www.jkp.com/catalogue/book/9781849057684/resources). It wasn't so much about what Henry ate because, given the limited options, I could remember that off the top of my head. It was more about how much he ate, what time he ate, where he was and what was happening around him, and, crucially, what sort of mood he was in. Our diary revealed Henry's need for calm and quiet both in his environment and in himself. I noticed that he ate better after exercise when his body was relaxed, and he also ate with less investigation when he was allowed to read at the table. 'Reading teas', we call them. The distraction seemed to take the pressure off, as no social skills were required. So when I first started to introduce new foods, we read *The Adventures of Tintin* as an accompaniment. It's just lucky that I happen to be an Hergé fan because we read those books a lot and I can now recite them pretty much word for word.

Henry would get really keyed up before mealtimes and often spent ages in the bathroom repeatedly washing his hands or feeling the need to arrange his toys perfectly before he sat down. I suppose this was displacement activity – doing something comforting and familiar when he felt most stressed. What was adding to that stress was my timekeeping, as I'm always cramming too much in, wanting to get on with it and then on to the next thing. That approach of 'Let's have lunch and then we'll...' was pressure that just exacerbated the issues that Henry had with his food. So I started planning in extra time for mealtimes and, more often than not, serving Henry ten minutes ahead of everybody else. And what do you know? I had a calmer, happier boy.

It is also a good idea, I think, once you have done a load of information gathering about your child's eating habits, that you make a visit to your family doctor, even if it is only to be told that there is nothing else going on. I know that some medicines can affect appetite and digestion, and if your child suffers acid reflux or constipation, they may associate eating with discomfort. So getting the all-clear from your doctor is a great idea.

Things you already know

Stick to a set mealtime routine: three good-sized meals a day with maybe two snack breaks. It helps regulate blood sugar levels and a hungry Asperger has huge control issues. And why should they have to deal with that? Try eating the same kind of food on the same day of the week. There's comfort knowing that it is fish on Fridays.

Pandering to Asperger sensibilities is the route to better mealtimes. An obvious one is the need for routine. For instance, we have the same preamble to each meal: exercise, downtime and wash hands. Henry has his place at the table set with his favourite mug, the right cutlery and the same chair (he'll notice if they get switched around). We have hard-backed dining chairs and Henry would squirm about, partly through not wanting to be there but also because he needed the sensory distraction. A firm cushion to push against went some way to solving that one. Think memory foam!

Self-preservation

Some days don't fight it; give in and know it's OK. Serve everybody dinner in front of a film. (We like David Attenborough's *First Life*.) Maybe throw in a small bribe: 'Eat your broccoli first and then we will turn the film on.' And give yourself a break. It's so easy to get wound up by a child who won't eat. It doesn't do your digestion any good at all. Many's a time I have paced round the garden, glass of wine in hand, swearing to myself, willing Nice Mummy to make an appearance, my dinner congealing in the dining room. Those days are not over. There are just going to be fewer of them. But know you are trying. Know you are doing your best. And breathe. It's going to be all right.

chapter 2

No-Battle Breakfast

Giving your Asperger the best start to their day involves thinking outside the cereal box. Breakfast – literally to *break the night-time fast* – is the most important meal of the day, but it is ten times more so for an Asperger. Left to their own devices at school, they may revert to safe, nutrient-poor foods. So getting vitamins, minerals and protein into your child at the start of the day will aid good behaviour and maintain energy levels and attention. An Asperger starting out on processed carbohydrate and sugary cereal is pretty much guaranteed a day of mood swings, bad behaviour and lack of concentration. Take the effort you would put into making a delicious dinner, double it and focus on *breakfast*. Think protein. We are talking eggs, meat, fish and dairy. Protein stabilizes, calms and nourishes. Chez Patten, we have progressed from dry cereal to scrambled eggs, fish cakes and ham steaks with apple slices or carrots on the side. Top favourite: French toast.

Mornings can be trying. We have had the same routine *every morning* for the last seven years and it's still not a smooth process. Henry doesn't corner-turn from one activity to another well at all. So I have taken one awkward transition out of our morning and I give him his breakfast in bed. Sounds ridiculously indulgent, but it takes about half the stress out of my morning too because he doesn't have to go anywhere to get breakfast. And once he's eaten it, the trajectory to the bathroom and then to get dressed is an easy one. He starts off with a glass of warm water to rehydrate and (ahem) get things going. TMI, I know. But it does make for a better school day.

The easiest, no-stress way to start to give your child a better breakfast is to make what looks like his go-to bland carbohydrate but make it a five-star version. The next step is to introduce a small piece of first-class protein such as egg or bacon, serving it alongside the carbohydrate. The aim is to start carb-based, but slowly reduce the amount of carbohydrate as you increase the protein until the protein takes centre stage. Here are our all-time favourite breakfasts, starting out carb-based and moving to protein-based. What these breakfasts all have in common, and why Henry will eat them, is that they all have a consistent texture: no skins, pips, squishy bits and no sloppy stuff mixing liquid and solid. Serving Henry's breakfast in a large flat-based pasta bowl allows the various constituents of the breakfast sufficient space without bothering their neighbour and means that they are unlikely to slide off on to the bed when he turns the page of his current novel.

WHOLEWHEAT PANCAKES

ingredients

For the pancakes

- 1 cup (100g) wholewheat flour
- ⅓ cup (30g) ground almonds
- 3 tsp baking powder
- Pinch salt
- 2 tsp sugar
- 1 large egg
- ¾ cup (200ml) whole milk
- 2 tbsp melted butter
- Butter for pan

Sides

Good-quality unsmoked back bacon with the fatty end cut off and fried gently. Sausage, peanut butter or turkey slices are also favourites.

Method

In a large bowl, mix the flour, almonds, baking powder, salt and sugar; in another smaller bowl, whisk the egg, milk and melted butter. Gradually add the egg, milk and butter mixture to the flour and sugar mixture, and whisk together thoroughly. Heat a large frying pan with a little butter over a medium heat. I use a hefty-bottomed frying pan, not the non-stick variety because I am suspicious of Teflon. I also transfer the batter to a jug and pour the batter on to the frying pan because I get into a terrible mess with spoons and ladles. Pour enough out until the pancake spreads to about 4" (10cm) across. When the surface bubbles and the edges are a light brown, flip over. The ground almonds make the pancakes deliciously squidgy. And the best bit is that your child won't know it's in there!

Start off by serving the pancakes by themselves until they become familiar. With pancakes, this shouldn't take too long! Then add in a small piece of bacon on a separate plate or maybe half a sausage or a small spoonful of peanut butter. These have to be eaten as part of the breakfast.

For as long as you like, combine a favoured carbohydrate with a small amount of first-class protein. Then over time increase the amount of the protein and reduce the amount of the carbohydrate. So instead of serving pancakes with a bit of bacon on the side, you're serving bacon with a pancake on the side, or buttered eggs with cornbread on the side.

Here are some more fortified carbohydrates.

BANANA MUFFINS

Banana muffins are the best because they look like cake (well, they sort of are), but mine are low in sugar and packed with protein; what's more, they take 30 minutes from start to serve. I used to blend the oats so they weren't at all obvious in the muffin, but now I don't bother because Henry's fine with the mixed texture. Also, a drop or two of vanilla added means you can get away with using less sugar. Not sure why but it works – possibly taste association! These are a brilliant easy breakfast option.

ingredients

- 1 cup (80g) porridge oats, blended into fine pieces
- 1 cup (250ml) whole milk
- 4 tbsp vegetable oil
- ¼ cup (30g) sugar
- 1 or 2 drops of natural vanilla essence

- 2 egg yolks, whisked
- 1 cup (125g) all-purpose flour
- 2 mashed ripe bananas
- 2 tsp baking powder

Method

To create an even-textured muffin, blitz the porridge oats with a hand blender or in a food processor until the pieces are smaller and will meld into the mixture unobtrusively. Don't get carried away, though, and end up with oat flour! Pour the milk on the oats and soak for 10 minutes. Meanwhile, whisk the oil, the sugar, vanilla and egg yolks together. Then add the flour, banana and baking powder, and finally the oat mixture.

Preheat the oven to 425°F/220°C/200°C fan/gas mark 7. Grease a muffin tray with a little butter and then spoon the mixture in, filling each hole two-thirds of the way up. Bake for approximately 15–20 minutes until a skewer inserted in the centre of a muffin comes out clean.

BITE-SIZE OATY PANCAKES

Here's another pancake recipe with a large dollop of disguised protein actually in the pancake, provided by the oats and yoghurt. Feel free to add chopped apple, banana, berries or whatever your child is ready to eat.

I blast the quick oats to make them smaller and not as noticeable in the finished pancake. Because they are pre-cooked, they are absorbed more easily into the mixture, but regular oats also work.

ingredients

- 1 cup (125g) wholewheat flour
- ½ cup (40g) quick-cooking oats, blasted in a spice mill or grinder for a few seconds
- Pinch salt
- 2 tsp baking powder
- 1 large egg
- 1 cup (250ml) milk
- 1 tbsp raw brown sugar
- ¼ cup (60g) mild full-fat Greek yoghurt
- 2–3 drops vanilla extract
- Knob of butter

Method

Mix the flour, oats, salt and baking powder in a large bowl. In another smaller bowl, whisk the eggs, milk, brown sugar, yoghurt and vanilla. Then incorporate the flour mix gradually into the wet ingredients. Transfer the batter to a jug. Heat a heavy-based pan, oiled with a little butter, on a medium heat and pour out the batter. Smaller pancakes work better with this oaty mixture. When bubbling and turning golden round the edges, flip over and cook for another 2 minutes. We eat these with smoked salmon, sausage, bacon and turkey slices, all on the side but not all at once!

CORN BREAD

Corn bread is packed with fibre and wholegrain and very much enjoyed by a hungry child of a cold morning. Goes very well with a chunk of ham, turkey or peanut butter on the side.

ingredients

- 1¼ cups (150g) all-purpose flour
- 1½ cups (225g) cornmeal or polenta
- Pinch salt

- 3 tsp baking powder
- 1 tbsp sugar
- ¾ cup (200ml) whole milk
- 3 eggs
- ½ stick (50g) melted butter

Method

Grease an 8" (20cm) square baking tin with butter. Preheat the oven to 450°F/230°C/210°C fan/gas mark 8. Mix all the ingredients thoroughly in a large bowl and then pour into the buttered tin. Bake on the middle shelf for about 25 minutes. It is ready when it is springy to the touch. Leave to cool in the tin and cut into squares.

Trading places

After a number of weeks or months, when you successfully have meat and eggs forming the majority of the breakfast, it is time to expand that protein repertoire. 'Buttered eggs', as Henry calls them, was our own first protein-based breakfast, the naming of which is a result of reading too much *Swallows and Amazons* and *Just William*. Not a bad thing. We like trad in our house. A hefty plate of eggs for breakfast was the single most important food introduction we made, because it had the instant effect of massively improving Henry's ability to concentrate at school. And that was huge.

BUTTERED EGGS

Buttered eggs are very simple. Melt a knob of butter in a frying pan on a low heat. Whisk the eggs in a bowl. I always do two per child and one for luck. Pour eggs into the pan and shuffle them about with a wooden spatula until they reach the required consistency. Henry happens to like his rather rubbery with a slice of toast on the side. I usually team the eggs up with a sliced apple in a separate bowl.

Henry sits in bed quite happily reading and eating, with only the occasional reminder to finish up and get into the bathroom. I give him half an hour to eat his breakfast before the chivvying starts to get him to the point of leaving on time for school.

For the longest time Henry would really only eat his eggs buttered. When, aged eight, he went visiting his friend Griffin, Griffin's mother asked Henry how he would like his eggs cooked and he replied with a look of indignation, 'The usual way!' To Henry, there was only one way of cooking eggs. Now, aged 11, we have three ways of cooking breakfast eggs: hard boiled, as an omelette and buttered. That's progress for you. Breaking into omelettes was a breeze because they are pretty much a solid version of buttered and he would eat them with bacon on the side. The transition from buttered to boiled was achieved by getting Henry to make both forms one lunchtime to convince him that the two quite different manifestations of egg originated from the same source.

Once hard-boiled and peeled, initially he wouldn't eat the yolk and white together and they had to be separated. I also had to locate the spiral chalaza that suspends the yolk in the white because its stringiness if detected in the white would be very bad news indeed. It took two years before Henry ate a whole hard-boiled egg, aged nine. Even today, Henry will not consider, for a single moment, eating a soft-boiled egg and has to leave the room when his brother is dunking the soldiers and licking runny yolk off his fingers!

As eggs were happily accepted as breakfast, I introduced French toast, combining the texture of the bread and the egg, and this has become an all-time breakfast favourite.

FRENCH TOAST

French toast mornings are always really good ones. The best French toast is made with white fluffy farmhouse but it doesn't contain the protein and wholegrain goodness that brown bread does. So we mix it up – some days brown, some white. This is a great breakfast to progress to after buttered eggs and toast because it is actually the perfect marriage of the two.

ingredients (for 2 boys)

- 4 eggs
- Knob of butter for the pan
- 4 thick slices of day-old bread (the drier it is, the more it soaks up the egg)

Method

Whisk your eggs for a minute to make sure they are well blended and then pour into a large, shallow casserole dish that will neatly contain the four slices of bread. I use one egg per slice of bread. If the bread is super-spongy, add a couple more eggs – they won't go to waste. Place the slices of bread flat in the dish and give them a good 20 minutes to soak, turning at half-time. Warm a large buttered frying pan and place the French toast slices carefully in the pan. Gently press them down until they squeak to get the bottoms evenly cooked. After a minute, when the bottom is brown, turn them over and cook on the other side. Extra egg can be drizzled on top while they cook. As an accompaniment, try turkey slices, ham, bacon, apple slices.

other protein options

Sausages quickly became one of our breakfast staples, but initially Henry would only eat frankfurters as they didn't really have skins and had the desired even consistency – certainly no herby or fatty bits. I did grapple with my conscience about feeding hot dogs to my growing son because I was brought up to believe that all the leftover nasty bits of a pig and other unmentionables were ground down to make frankfurters. So I scoured the supermarkets and eventually found some wholesome ones with a high meat content that also happened to be organic. Fantastic!

Fish makes a wonderful start to the day and couldn't be easier to prepare: just fry it. We started with the milder ones such as halibut and coley but quickly worked up to salmon. (I avoid fish with small bones such as trout because I can't guarantee getting them all out.) Think of all those amazing omegas feeding your child's brilliant growing brain. You may expect that stuffing Henry with fried fish and eggs every morning has made him a real fatty, but he's a veritable string bean. (Just looks like one. Wouldn't eat them until he was about nine.) Protein and fat fill you up and therefore I reckon children are less likely to snack on sugary processed rubbish that seems to be the real culprit for piling the weight on.

I had hoped to move Henry on to porridge and oatmeal, but no luck there. He would eat Weetabix under duress, but that didn't pan out as the milk unevenly changed the Weetabix's character – and not for the better in Henry's opinion. Warm milk on Weetabix was just too yucky to contemplate.

FiSHCAKES

Fishcakes seem like a big deal for breakfast, but in actual fact they only take 5 minutes to put together, especially if you use tinned fish or fillets you have prepped the night before. Usually, fishcakes are a texture challenge for Aspies, but ours are very simple and leave out all the undesirable elements.

ingredients

- ½ cup (250g) fresh or tinned fish (start with a mild fish and work up to stronger-flavoured ones)
- 1 medium-sized potato, boiled and mashed
- 2 egg yolks
- 1 tbsp all-purpose flour
- Pinch salt
- ½ stick (50g) butter for the pan

Method

How you make your fishcakes is really down to what your child will eat. Here's my basic version with the minimum of potato to help with the consistency (Henry didn't accept mashed potato until he was ten) and egg to bind the lot. Start by taking a cooked fillet of coley. Flake it into a bowl and use a fork to blend it thoroughly with the mashed potato, egg yolks, flour and salt. Press the mixture with your hands into small cakes, roll in flour to coat the edges and put them in the fridge while the butter heats in the pan. I use butter to cook almost everything because it is a taste that Henry likes; with frying, however, you have to make sure that it gets hot enough to cook well but doesn't overheat and burn, which will affect the taste of the fishcakes. Place the fishcakes gently in the hot butter and fry each side for 5–10 minutes depending on their size. Wait until the bottoms are properly browned before turning; otherwise, they do have a tendency to fall to bits! Fishcakes are possibly our all-round best breakfast so far. Maybe add a few slices of apple. Perfect.

MINUTE MINI STEAKS

A steak in the morning may seem a little heavy, but that first-class protein is exactly what your child needs. It's fast and tasty, and gets the brain going in double quick time. Also super-filling and satisfying, it will keep their concentration up all the way to lunchtime.

I take a nice cut of beef and use a good sharp knife to slice it to make many little thin steaks of about ¼" (½cm) thick. Sometimes you can buy steak cut for stir-fry and that will save you even more time. Heat a pan on high with a splash of olive or sunflower oil. When the oil is smoking, place the pieces of meat in the pan, taking care to have the whole of one side in contact with the pan to ensure that they cook evenly. After half a minute, working through the fillets in the same order you set them down in the pan, turn them over, pressing the steaks firmly on to the pan with a spatula. You don't want to overcook the steaks, but, for the sake of achieving an even texture, they must be cooked through. Flip them out of the pan on to a cooled plate and serve with a slice of warm toast and a raw carrot.

Once you have got your head around cooking dinner-style meat for breakfast, go ahead and try anything and everything that looks good. Be adventurous and encourage your child to try all kinds of protein. We've had duck, lamb and even venison before 8.00am. By the way, I do hope that you are not cooking up all this great protein for your child for breakfast and then helping yourself to a bowl of Special K. Mums too can very much benefit from a protein-rich start to the day. Research at the University of Missouri[1] showed that a little over an ounce (35g) of protein eaten first thing increased brain activity by 30 per cent in adults and caused significant weight loss. So you'll be smarter and thinner. What's not to love!

---

1   H. J. Leidy, L. C. Ortinau, S. M. Douglas and H. A. Hoertel (2013) 'Beneficial effects of a higher-protein breakfast on the appetitive, hormonal, and neural signals controlling energy intake regulation in overweight/obese, "breakfast-skipping," late-adolescent girls.' *American Journal of Clinical Nutrition 97*, 4, 677–688.

Chapter 3

Skipping Lunch is for Sissies

Part 1: School

Packed and ready to go

The thing with lunches is that for a school-aged child they are usually eaten away from you. So the challenge here is not so much about getting your child to consume good nutritious fodder as setting them up so that they are able to focus sufficiently to eat anything at all. Dining halls at school are noisy, busy places with bright fluorescent lights, clanging cutlery and pungent smells, all a major assault on an Asperger's senses. Henry likened the school dining hall to entering a warzone with missiles coming at him from all sides. The food served isn't always Asperger-friendly either.

Up until the age of seven, Henry had pretty much avoided eating lunch at school. In pre-school he only stayed a half-day, and from aged four to seven he attended a progressive Steiner school in the Midwest, where school was out at 2.00pm. Henry got through his day snacking on bread and crackers and drinking pints and pints of milk.

I suppose knowing then that Henry was about to go up a year, where the school day extended to 3.30pm, went some way to focusing my attentions on his limited diet and just how that would sustain my rapidly growing boy for an extra hour and a half a day. When the next school year did come around, I gave him a week or so of the new daily regime with his usual bread, crackers and milk, and then I thought that perhaps he would bow to peer pressure and ease into lunching with the other kids. This was a private school and the food selections were like that of a mid-class hotel, with plenty of kid-friendly fare on offer. I also had a theory (for about a minute) that away from the tensions and expectations of home – that is, *me* – and without the comforting carbs packed for him, he would be weaned off this bland eating fad, connect with other children around him and, after a while, eat what they ate. For one dreadful week we persisted with this experiment. But Henry really couldn't deal with having school lunches on any level and the distress it caused him was awful. So when I began to focus seriously on his relationship with food and we turned our dietary corner, that's when we embraced single-texture packed lunches Asperger-style! Eaten, of course, in the quietest seats at the back of the dining hall.

It has to be noted here that making the lunch situation work was entirely down to the good connections I had built up over a couple of years with teachers and the Principal. I pretty soon realized when Henry started school that my role as mother was to be extended to include being his PR. Teachers are busy people with a lot coming at them from all sides. And I fully appreciate their position. No teacher Henry has ever had has received ASD training; so when they see him acting out, that's all they see and he's marked down as odd and a trouble-maker. It has been my job to decode this behaviour, pointing out the triggers and the whys, and then share my management tools, allowing the teachers to see the clever, inquisitive, polite child, not the annoying, soon-to-be-certified one.

My advice is to do the same: work at your relationship with your child's teachers and give something back by helping out with the school in whatever way you can. Otherwise, the only interaction you may get with your child's teacher is when there's a problem, usually a problem that's been allowed to get out of hand, and then you are starting out on the back foot. Build up that relationship before there's an issue to address and you'll find that small, informal comments from the teacher can head off potential problems. Let your child's teacher know that what you want is for your child to be a good student and you wish to work with her (or him) to help make that happen. For us it was small tweaks that made big changes: sitting Henry at the front of the class where he could see the teacher and the board without intermediate visual distraction; giving him a pressure ball to squeeze to stay calm; tolerating, if at all possible, the constant tapping of his fingers and feet, because he needs to do that to sit still. The main message to reinforce, sent carefully and clearly, is: treat him kindly and with respect. Harsh comments hit deep, and even if you see no perceptible change in his manner, those comments will be processed later and cause pain. If other students see a teacher's less-than-kind treatment of him, they will take that as permission to also treat him badly. Above all, let the teacher know that this is a two-way relationship and what she/he puts into your child, they will get back several fold. And remember that a happy child will eat a better diet and in turn be able to function and focus at school.

Cold Lunch options

My aim initially was to enforce a positive school dining experience by giving Henry a lunch that seemingly replicated the bland foods he craved. And here are some fortified breads and cakes that are nutritional powerhouses in disguise. I might warn you that these attractive-looking carbs won't taste quite the way you're expecting – indeed, they won't win any taste tests, period. But they will be accepted and eaten by a hungry child at lunchtime who believes that Mummy has given him a lovely piece of normal, regular, everyday bread to eat. And that's all they need to know.

Here's a bread that's got masses of protein with the egg, wholewheat flour and soya. Soya flour comes with an impressive list of nutrients such as iron, potassium and phosphorus, but what it also has, along with the wholewheat flour, is a mineral that I think is really important and that's magnesium. Magnesium, according to the National Institutes of Health,[1] is key to the transmission of nerve signals and contributes to a healthy immune response, in addition to many other essential functions. Some neuropathic and homeopathic doctors also claim that many of the symptoms of ASD kids are a function of chronic magnesium deficiency because either it is lacking in their diet or their intestine is unable to absorb it.[2] I am not sure how far I go along with that one, but I do notice a distinct improvement in my child's overall demeanour when he's eating a diet rich in leafy green vegetables, brown rice and protein. So it does make sense to me that a mineral responsible for calming the nervous system and relaxing the mind should be pretty much top of the list in desirables to incorporate into our children's diet. Other high-magnesium foods are broccoli and almonds, which is why broccoli was a great first vegetable to incorporate into Henry's diet and why I love to heap almond flour into as many cake recipes as I possibly can. Pumpkin seeds are also extremely rich in magnesium, so feel free to switch out a tablespoon of flour for ground pumpkin seeds in any cake recipe to give them a marvellous magnesium boost.

SOYA BREAD

A lovely rich bread that is highly nutritious and will be accepted by a child with Asperger's whose food of choice is even-textured carbohydrate. Use this better-grade bread to form the basis of your early lunches and then, as with the breakfasts, slowly reduce the quantity of it in favour of protein and vegetables. I sent Henry to school with a

---

1   National Institutes of Health, Office of Dietary Supplements (2013) 'Magnesium: Fact Sheet for health professionals.' Bethesda, MD: National Institutes of Health. Available at http://ods.od.nih.gov/factsheets/Magnesium-HealthProfessional/#en1, accessed on 16 September 2014.

2   B. Rimland (1987) 'Megavitamin B6 and Magnesium in the Treatment of Autistic Children and Adults.' In E. Schopler and G. B. Mesibov (eds) *Neurobiological Issues in Autism*, pp.389–405. New York: Plenum Press.

chunk of homemade bread and a piece of chicken breast along with milk in a flask for what seemed like for ever before introducing added extras. More of them later.

ingredients

- 2 tsp raw brown sugar
- ½oz (14g/2 sachets) dried yeast
- ¾ cup (200ml) tepid water
- 3 cups (400g) wholewheat bread flour

- ⅔ cup (100g) soya flour
- Pinch salt
- 1 large egg, beaten
- Mild-flavoured oil

Method

Take the sugar, yeast and half of the water and mix together in a cup or small jug and leave in a warm place for about 20 minutes until frothy. Use this time to grease a 1lb (450g) loaf tin. Then combine the flours and salt in a large bowl and add the yeast mixture, the egg and the rest of the water. Mix together with a fork into a soft dough.

On a floured surface, knead the dough by folding the top edge over into the middle of the dough and pressing it down with your knuckles, then turning the dough 90° before folding over again. Repeat this action for at least 10 minutes until the dough feels springy and elastic; then place it back in the bowl and cover with a damp tea towel or oil-coated Saran Wrap/cling film. Place the bowl in a warm place to rise (an airing cupboard or a sunny spot in your kitchen is perfect) for about an hour or until it has doubled in size. Next, take the risen dough and bash all the air out of it, kneading it again for 5 minutes on a floured surface. Shape the dough and place into the greased loaf tin. Brush the top of the loaf with a mild-flavoured oil and place again in a warm spot for around 15 minutes until the dough has risen to the top of the tin. Bake on the middle shelf at 350°F/180°C/160°C fan/gas mark 4 for 35–45 minutes. To check if the loaf is cooked inside, take it out of the tin and tap the base: it should sound hollow. If it is ready, sit the bread on a wire rack to cool.

QUINOA BREAD

Quinoa is the answer to so many of our dietary prayers. Dubbed the Incan super-grain, quinoa is jam-packed with protein, iron, magnesium, manganese and B2, all in a useful high-fibre package. The actual grain, cooked on its own, has a texture beyond Henry's current comfort zone, but I have combined it here in a bread and it works very well. I find using the flour in bread, even mixed with conventional flours, makes the bread heavy and robust. This superior bread is light and highly nutritious. When I first made this bread, as with the other oat recipes, I used to give the oats and quinoa a quick blast with a hand blender to even up their texture.

ingredients

- ¼oz (7g/1 sachet) dried yeast
- 1¼ cups (300ml) tepid water
- 1 tbsp honey
- 1 tbsp vegetable oil
- 3 tbsp powdered milk
- 1 cup (160g) quinoa grain, cooked in 1¾ cups (450ml) water for 15 minutes or until all the water is absorbed (if necessary add a little more water and cook for an extra minute or two until the grain is plump and soft)
- ½ cup (30g) oats, cooked in ⅔ cup (50ml) milk for 10 minutes or until all the milk is absorbed
- 3 cups (370g) white bread flour
- 1 cup (100g) wholewheat flour
- 2 pinches salt
- Mild-flavoured oil

Method

In a small bowl, add the yeast to the tepid water and honey; leave for 20 minutes until frothy and then thoroughly mix in the oil and powdered milk. Combine the quinoa and oats in a large bowl. Add the yeast mixture to the quinoa and oats, and finally fold in the white bread flour, wholewheat flour and salt until it forms a nice elastic dough. Follow the instructions for kneading and baking in the soya bread recipe above.

SCOTTISH OAT CAKES

The gluten in oats seems to be better tolerated than other glutens by the Asperger children we know. But this recipe can be made with gluten-free oats that are now readily available in most large supermarkets. These wonderful savoury cakes are easy to make and give your child the comfort food they crave while upping their nutrient intake. Oats deliver loads of fibre, which is absolutely key for children who eat a diet lacking fruit and vegetables.

Oats also have a stabilizing effect on blood sugar, again aiding mood control.

ingredients

- 3 cups (250g) oats (blended to fine oatmeal)
- Pinch salt
- ½ tsp bicarbonate of soda
- ¼ stick (25g) melted butter
- ⅔ cup (150ml) hot water

Method

Mix together the oatmeal, salt and bicarbonate in a large bowl. Add the butter and hot water, stirring with a wooden spoon, and then use your hands to form a soft ball of dough. Lightly flour a clean worktop, roll the dough out to a ¼" (½cm) thickness and then use a cookie cutter or a glass to cut out the cakes. Bake on a greased baking tray at 375°F/190°C/170°C fan/gas mark 5 for approximately 20 minutes. Cool on a wire rack.

ALMOND CAKE

This is a basic version of a low-sugar almond cake that is loved beyond words in our household. It is also a great recipe to start simple and then add other ingredients as a way of expanding your child's taste and texture repertoire. We first introduced apple, thin slivers of peach, finely grated carrot and even finely grated zucchini/courgette with the skin removed so the green bits can't be spotted. Try anything else to add fibre and nutrients that you feel you can get away with. I knew we had cracked the texture thing when last week Henry ate this very cake with roughly smashed pumpkin seeds mixed in amongst it. It took four years to get there but it was worth it! The honey, incidentally, has an intense sweetness that allows less sugar to be used in this recipe.

ingredients

- 2 sticks (225g) softened butter
- ½ cup (100g) honey
- ½ cup (100g) sugar
- Finely grated lemon zest (optional)
- 2¼ cups (225g) ground almonds
- 3 large eggs
- ⅔ cups (125g) polenta or cornmeal
- 2 tsp baking powder
- Pinch salt

Method

Preheat the oven to 375°F/160°C/140°C fan/gas mark 3 and grease and line a 9" (22cm) round cake tin with melted butter and baking parchment. In a large bowl, beat the butter, honey, sugar and, if using it, lemon zest together until creamy. Stir in the almonds and then beat in the eggs one at a time. Then thoroughly mix in the polenta, baking powder and salt. Spoon the mixture into the tin and bake for about 50 minutes or until a skewer inserted in the centre of the cake comes out clean. Let the cake cool in the tin.

This type of bread or cake in your child's lunch box is a cut above the average version, but it is also a bribe for something better. So a small neat note in the lid of Henry's lunch box will say, 'Eat the carrot/broccoli/small pot of peanut butter to have your bread/cake.' These foods had previously been introduced at home and so were not a total surprise when he opened his lunch box. I'm happy to report that this bribery works most of the time. Some afternoons the vegetable and cake came home as a protest, but over time that happened less and less. Of course, the single broccoli floret or carrot stick, with some trial and error, multiplied into several carrot sticks, many mini broccoli florets, apple slices and green beans. I would have loved to have given him grapes, tomatoes, peppers, blueberries, cucumber and a myriad of fabulous and tasty fresh foods, but they just wouldn't have been eaten because they were still on the 'hated' list. I had to be careful with my lunchtime introductions because anything in there that he particularly took offence to – say, a broad bean – would completely put Henry off eating even his favourite foods and he'd come home in a complete state with a definite sense of betrayal. It's also not a pleasant thing unpacking a child's lunch box of bruised, sweaty fruit and veg. Quite apart from anything else, it's such a waste of money. I did try making soup from the homecoming vegetables but really couldn't face eating it. So we play safe with fruit and veg in packed lunches.

The great divide

Henry has always had his meals at home separated to a greater or lesser degree using either an array of small plates or a very large platter with pieces of food sitting miles apart like small tropical islands in a blue and white Spode sea. Henry has – or rather mostly *had* – a great fear that if the foods touched, they would contaminate each other. Whilst separate and pure, he would happily consume them, but if, say, a carrot stick should roll over and nestle by the chicken, in Henry's mind, cells and textures were traded, the meal was rendered inedible and hysterics would ensue.

So how to keep food happily apart in a packed lunch? When Henry did eventually get to be more relaxed about mixing foods, he felt comfortable with the elements of his lunch wrapped in foil. Boy, did we get through the foil, and yes, I reused it if I could. Before foil-wrapped lunches, we obsessively hunted for containers, not necessarily sold as lunch boxes, with compartments that allowed that neat segregation of food. Japanese bento boxes are the best, with many and varied compartments. But if you are buying one, be sure you buy a box meant to be carried and with a locking lid because the regular sort of bento boxes, even though they come with lids, won't stop the food from mixing about if the box is tipped in a bag. Failing that, there are craft organizers with small compartments and locking lids. I found a great draper's organizer, 8" (20cm) long, with different sized compartments and two levels. Small toolboxes are also wonderful, usually with two or more layers, sectioned-off spaces and sturdy catches that lock with a satisfying click. Do be careful, though, if you buy a metal one; don't place food directly on to the metal; wrap it in foil or waxed paper. Anything not made specifically for food shouldn't come directly in contact with it – although I did find a brilliant toolbox the other day with a built-in lunch section. Failing all that, strips of cereal box cardboard make very effective dividers in a lunch box and you get to choose where they go!

More cold Lunches

Henry's meat of choice is plain chicken breast meat. So I started packing his lunch with a smaller bread chunk and adding strips of cooked chicken wrapped in wax paper in one of his lunch box compartments. And then I bought sliced chicken normally used for sandwiches and made the slices into rolls, cutting the ends off and slicing the roll so they sat in the lunch box compartment neatly on their ends like mini bolts of fabric on an upholsterer's display. This you can do with any sliced meat. Presented in his lunch box exactly the same way, in the same compartment, one day I switched out a roll of chicken for turkey, then ham, Quorn slices, roast beef and bacon. What these meats have in common is a mild flavour and a consistent texture, and that gradually extended the meaty tastes that were acceptable to him. And for the same reason, salami, prosciutto, corned beef and tongue didn't work for Henry. We actually never even discussed the change of meat because, as far as he was concerned, they were all a type of chicken. Weeks later, of course, I would mention that he had ham in his lunch and Henry would initially respond negatively until he realized that he had in fact been eating ham on and off for the last two months!

This dubious approach is really all about training the taste buds to accept a new food without it visually registering as foreign. Going under the radar, as it were, is one of my main methods for expanding the diet. If you can get past that instant visual rejection, then it is a lot easier to get new foods in there.

Sliced meat rolls in their waxed paper overcoats were absolutely brilliant as the mainstay of Henry's lunch for quite some time. The teachers noticed a massive improvement in his concentration and behaviour. That protein at lunchtime gave him the best chance of a controlled and emotionally stable afternoon. As we explored more foods at home, so his school lunches became more varied. In fact, if he would eat something at dinner, I made sure I saved some for his next day's lunch. This made my life easier and cut down on the morning lunch prep. Try it for yourself: when you are cooking dinner, throw in another lamb chop, duck breast or couple of sausages for the next day's packed lunch. Once cooled, wrap the meat in foil and put it in the freezer overnight. That way it stays fresh and, if packed up around seven-ish, will be defrosted in time for lunch. It also helps keep the contents of the lunch box cool.

Cold drinks

A good water bottle, in your child's favourite colour, is so very important. We love metal ones, mainly because they are durable; over the years ours have developed quite a personality with all the knocks and bangs, but they are still perfectly serviceable. Plastic water bottles give me the willies as there's so much evidence about the nasty effect of degrading plastic leaching into the contents of the bottle. I encourage Henry to sip water through the day. More of that later.

It is a good idea to also provide a lunchtime drink, which offers an opportunity to add extra nutrients to your child's meal, especially if you are finding it hard to incorporate new foods into their diet. In the first few weeks of Henry's extended school day I added a liquid vitamin to his lunchtime milk, one especially formulated for children. Buy an unflavoured one or a mild flavour such as vanilla so it doesn't affect the taste of the milk. At age seven and eight, these additional vitamins worked fantastically well and I saw an immediate improvement in Henry's mental and physical wellbeing.

A sturdier version of our fortified milk is a protein shake which would definitely pack a bigger nutrient punch, but I found that Henry would drink the shake, feel too full and leave his 'proper' food. Plus, I really want him to *eat* a lunch, not *drink* it. That's just my preference. (See Chapter 5 on snacks and drinks, as we do use shakes to boost us out of that between-meal slump.) So we stick with the fortified milk and occasionally I switch cow's for almond, rice or oat milk, masking their taste by adding the tiniest drop of chocolate milk. Henry finds soya milk too weird and I have to say I am with him on that one. I don't pack him juice boxes or regular juice because the fructose is so high it makes him jittery, so I include a watered-down version, usually apple.

Hot drinks

A great cocoa is the very best winter drink, isn't it? Henry takes a much-loved narrow flask with cocoa made from whole milk mixed with a syrup of raw cocoa powder and a little agave. I don't like hot chocolate mixes because they contain salt, flavourings and stacks of sugar. That's pretty much it for hot drinks.

Favourite kit for packed lunches

We really came into our own when we discovered that packed lunches for Henry need not be an ever-repeated round of turkey rolls and carrot sticks. It all became a lot more fun when we discovered the delights of camping gadgetry. Henry developed an excitement and a focus on lunch because he'd get to use his special lunch kit. The multi-task tools and foldaway spoons that came in their own special pouch or hidden in flask lids added a whole techy, spy, James Bond theme to lunches. Asperger heaven, especially as there is a definite knack to stowing this kit – like the concertinaed flask spoon that if folded the wrong way won't fit into its sprung-loaded slot. That's usually my problem when I can't get everything back together and, for fear of breaking it in sheer frustration, I need to ask for assistance from my 11-year-old son.

We have the knife, fork and spoon that all clip together and to do so they must be in order. There's a long, thin, lightweight flask with a top that partially unscrews to allow pouring from where the arrows indicate. Specific knowledge required here. An insulated cool bag is essential for hot summer days with many zipped compartments that might hold a secret single square of chocolate or a note from Mummy. Football and other fun themed ice packs are always a friendly bonus. And by far our most popular lunch container is a broad-mouthed food flask that affords many interesting lunch options, which are so much nicer to eat on a cold day, and has the added bonus of a lid with the aforementioned foldaway spoon.

Hot packed lunch recipes

QUINOA PASTA SHAPES IN OLIVE OIL

Quinoa, as I have mentioned, is one of the most protein-rich foods out there, high in iron, magnesium, B2 and lysine, essential for tissue growth and repair, and while Henry won't eat the grain, the flour can be used to make some of his favourite foods. You will be fairly horrified, however, at the price of quinoa flour compared with that of the grain. So I buy the dried grain and use a hand blender to make my own flour. A food processor, or a coffee or spice grinder, would also do the job. The other thing is that quinoa has a curious musty, grassy smell and a slightly bitter taste that somehow works OK in a bread or in a pasta served with a flavoursome sauce but can be a little bit too much when the pasta's served plain. The answer is to toast it: either the grain before you grind it or the flour, by laying it out on a tray and gently cooking it in the oven on the lowest setting. The longer you toast it, the sweeter the flavour.

This pasta is fantastic because it is a bland carbohydrate with masses of protein! We have had great success with quinoa pasta and it is very simple to make.

ingredients

- 2 egg yolks
- 1 cup (100g) quinoa flour
- ¼ cup (25g) tapioca flour or white bread flour
- Olive oil or butter to serve

Method

Combine the egg yolks and flours in a bowl and knead well until they form a dough. It should be smooth and firm and not at all sticky. If it won't form a dough, it is probably too dry, so add water drop by drop, kneading with the back of your hand until you get a nice, hard ball of dough. The test is to press it against a smooth work surface and it should come away cleanly. Add a bit more flour if you feel it's too sticky.

The next step is to cut the pasta into shapes. My favourite is farfalle or bowtie pasta, which is quick and easy and a shape children like. Start by dusting the worktop with tapioca flour and roll out your pasta dough until it's about ⅛" (3–4mm) deep. With a sharp knife, cut off a 1" (3cm) strip and then cut across the ends to tidy them up. A ravioli cutter, if you have one, will give your farfalle lovely frilly edges but otherwise just use a regular sharp knife to cut 2" (5cm) lengths along the pasta strip, giving you a row of pasta oblongs. Then, with your thumb and first two fingers of your hand, simply scrunch the middle of the pasta pieces so make a bow-tie shape.

I don't expect you'll be getting up a half-hour early to make these fresh, so I make a large batch the night before and lay them out on a floured tray covered with Saran Wrap/cling film (they will keep like that in the fridge for two or three days). In the morning, heat your flask up with hot water while you cook the pasta in boiling water for 2–3 minutes. Drain well and toss in a little bit of butter or olive oil, which stops the pasta sticking together and also helps your child feel full. This pasta has been a great lunchtime success for us because it is a safe, soft, bland food that Henry loves to eat and it has a secret supply of protein and nutrients, which is all rather fantastic. Use the tapioca flour to make this recipe gluten-free.

RiCE FRiTTERS

These rice fritters are perfect for lunch pots because they are small and easy to eat with a fork or fingers. They have a hefty protein content with the eggs but don't smell overtly eggy, always a consideration when eating at school. They suit my Asperger because they are fairly bland-tasting but have a chewy texture that Henry loves. It is quite a long-winded process but absolutely worth it, and you can make the fritters the day before and allow them to rise for a second time overnight in the fridge ready to be cooked in the morning.

ingredients

- ⅔ cup (100g) brown rice
- ⅛oz (3g/a little less than half a sachet) dried yeast
- 2 tbsp warm water
- 1 heaped tsp sugar
- 2 eggs, well beaten
- Pinch salt
- 3 tbsp all-purpose flour
- Mild-flavoured oil or butter for frying

Method

The softer the rice, the better the cakes, so slightly overcook the rice in salted water until it is really soft and then drain well. It helps to further dry the rice by laying it out on kitchen paper, rolling the kitchen paper over it and squeezing out any excess water. Transfer the rice to a good-sized bowl. In a small jug add the yeast and sugar to the warm water and put aside for 10 minutes. When the yeast is good and frothy, add it to the rice and use a wooden spoon to mix it all together thoroughly. Cover the bowl with Saran Wrap/cling film and leave the rice and yeast mixture in a warm place such as an airing cupboard or a sunny windowsill for about an hour and a half. It doesn't rise exactly like bread, but it does bulk out a bit. The next step is to mix in the beaten egg, salt and flour. Then either leave the batter for a further 15 minutes to rise again before cooking or put it in the fridge overnight to be cooked the following morning. The mixture should now have the consistency of thick rice pudding.

I shallow-fry these fritters in ½" (1cm) of vegetable oil, adding spoonfuls of batter evenly spaced in the oil, for a couple of minutes each side. The fritters should turn a lovely deep golden colour and are cooked through if they feel springy when you push a spatula down on the top. Failing that, take one out and cut it in half to check. I like small fritters so I use a dessertspoon which makes 2" (5cm) diameter cakes that fit neatly stacked in the food flask. Cook a small number at a time to keep the oil hot.

Remember to fill your food flask with boiling water to heat it up. Leave it for 5 minutes, drain and wipe out with a paper towel. Then fill your flask with rice fritters!

MiNi MEATBALLS

Single-textured and meaty, these will go down very well once your Aspie has made the move to proteins. I do prepare these the night before or even the week before and freeze them raw. After a night in the fridge, just take the meatballs out in the morning and cook for 10 minutes. These meatballs are wonderful for Asperger kids because the overriding texture is a meaty one and they are really easy to eat. Initially, try this recipe without the yeast extract, then add a little to subsequent batches and build up the amount your child will accept. The yeast extract is a marvellous concentrated hit of energy-boosting and stress-busting B-complex vitamins, which is a real help to ASDers, especially if they are having a tough time.

ingredients

- 1lb (500g) prime ground beef/pork/turkey/buffalo
- 2 cups (100g) wholewheat breadcrumbs
- 2 egg yolks

- Pinch salt
- 1 tsp yeast extract (optional)
- All-purpose flour for coating the raw meatballs
- Vegetable oil for frying

Method

To make these delicious mouth-sized, meaty treats, start by taking a large bowl and mix the ground meat with the breadcrumbs, which actually helps make them sturdy without altering the texture. Add the egg yolks, a pinch of salt and the yeast extract if you are using it. Thoroughly combine all the ingredients with clean hands and then form into small balls around 1" (3cm) in diameter. Roll in flour. If you are prepping these the night before, then set aside on a tray, cover with Saran Wrap/cling film and pop in the fridge. In the morning, take a heavy-based frying pan, add enough oil to cover a quarter of the meatball and bring the pan up to a good heat with the oil just smoking. While the oil is heating, boil the kettle and pour the hot water into your food flask to warm it up. Cook the meatballs for 5 minutes on each side and check a big one when you think they're cooked to see that there's no pink inside. Pour out the water from the flask, wipe the inside with a paper towel and fill with as many meatballs as you think your child will eat.

SLOW-COOKED LAMB

I love slow cooking as a no-stress way to prepare a leg of meat. Lamb works very well and sealing the meat ensures it stays succulent without the need for a sauce. Once Henry would tolerate foods touching, I found that I could pack the food flask half full with piping hot lamb and sit raw broccoli on top and by lunchtime nicely al dente broccoli was all ready to eat and bursting with goodness. Definitely a dish to be cooked for dinner and reheated for the lunch pot. It also works brilliantly as a cold meat for the bento box.

This is a version of an old French recipe that uses wine, of course, but we will use vegetable stock which works just as well.

ingredients

- 4 tbsp olive oil
- 2–2½lb (1–1.5kg) half leg of lamb on the bone (to fit into your casserole dish)
- Large pinch salt
- 6 large onions, sliced
- 3–4 pints (1.5–2 litres) vegetable stock (see next recipe)
- 1 level tbsp cornstarch

Method

Set your oven at 325°F/160°C/140°C fan/gas mark 3. You'll need a heavy-based stove-top-to-oven casserole dish with a tight-fitting lid. Heat the oil in the casserole and then rub a large pinch of salt over the lamb. When the oil is smoking, fry the leg of lamb all over for 10 minutes, making sure every bit is seared. Don't stint on this step because it really makes a difference, holding in the flavour of the meat. When all the sides are a lovely golden brown, remove the lamb from the casserole and place it on a dish to one side. Fry the onions for 3–4 minutes, then arrange over the bottom of the casserole. Place the lamb on the onions and cover entirely with the vegetable stock. Put the lid on, position it on the middle shelf of the oven and cook for 2 hours. After 2 hours, the meat should be falling off the bone and so tender you could cut it with a spoon. If that's not the case, bung it in for another 20 minutes, making sure the meat is still under the stock. The beautiful thing about cooking meat like this for an ASD child is that it is superbly soft, easy to eat and even-textured all the way through. Once cooked, set the meat to one side to further tenderize for 5 minutes. I then strain the cooking fluid, add the cornstarch and reduce it further for 10 minutes on the hob to make the most fantastic gravy.

The meat stays moist on the bone, so the next day simply carve off easy-to-eat chunks, zap in the microwave for 2 minutes or gently heat through in a little bit of the gravy, drain and place in a pre-warmed lunch pot.

SECRET SOUP

I have a boy who sucks down smoothies and drinks milk and juice as if they are going out of fashion, but runs screaming from a bowl of soup. Even broths without floaty bits or hidden vegetables lurking in the depths are deemed repulsive. But, as everyone knows, stocks and broths are a life force full of goodness. So I have taken to cooking rice, couscous and noodles in a broth, making what appears to be a very plain dish ten times more nutritious. Besides, I have always found it really satisfying to cook up a wholesome pot of vegetable, chicken or beef stock (I know, I need to get out more), especially when you can freeze batches of it for future use. Here's a basic recipe. I try whenever possible to use organic meat and vegetables because I would rather not have those chemical nasties in my stock.

Stock

Stock is so very useful for bolstering a whole range of recipes. Here it is the key to secret soup. No two stocks of mine taste the same because it isn't an accurate science, the main objective being to get as much goodness and flavour out of the meat and veggies as possible.

I really love to buy a chicken, take off most of the meat and then cook the carcass for stock. But if you have had a roast chicken dinner, a cooked one works nearly as well. A couple of years ago I invested in a stockpot and I absolutely love it. It is quite tall and sturdy and holds the heat well with a good lid, allowing the stock to bubble away nicely for hours on the lowest hob setting.

ingredients

- Cooked or raw chicken carcass/beef on the bone
- 4 leeks
- 4 large onions
- 3 cloves of garlic
- 6 medium carrots
- 6 stalks celery
- Pinch salt
- Sprig parsley (you can also add thyme and bay but they are omitted here because Henry doesn't like their flavour)

Method

Put all the ingredients into your stockpot or large pan and add enough water to cover the chicken or beef and veggies and then the same amount again, which will be somewhere around 4–5 pints (2–2.5 litres) of water, aiming to make 2–3 pints (1–1.5 litres) of stock. If this is to be just a vegetable stock, use one and a half times the quantities of vegetables with around 4 pints (2 litres) of water. Slowly bring the stock to the boil and, if it has chicken or beef, use a metal spoon to skim off any fat that floats to the surface. Turn the heat right down so the stock is barely simmering, put the lid on and leave to cook away for at least 3 hours. Strain the stock and then let it cool completely, once again removing any surface fat.

Take any dried food that requires rehydration and replace the water with your stock – just follow the instructions on the packet for couscous, dehydrated vegetable protein and so on. With pasta or any type of noodles (e.g. soba noodles) and rice, cook them just covered with the stock, keeping the lid on tight to ensure all the stock is absorbed, topping up the stock if need be.

So there you have it – lovely hot and cold nutritious packed lunches that go a long way to allowing our children to control their moods and behaviour so they can function better in class.

We all know that our children have unusual and special skills (ours are fact retention, mathematics and science), and I believe that good food suppresses aberrant behaviour and lets these special qualities shine through.

chapter 4

Skipping Lunch is For Sissies

Part 2: Home

Home front

Home lunches take on many forms and guises. There is the large, laid-back Sunday lunch, which is usually one of our famous mixed-dish extravaganzas with many Asperger-friendly options. There's the Saturday no-stress lunch between activities or out and about on trips. And then there are holiday lunches, special family lunches and lunches for boys who are at home feeling sicky. For us, lunch is never skipped, light or a quick bite, because what is eaten can pretty much dictate how the afternoon goes and whether we happily make it to dinner.

The lunches in this chapter, like all our meals, are anchored in protein, be it duck, burger or ham, with as many vegetables as I can get in there! All *single*-texture, working up to *simple*-texture stuff. Start by giving your child a piece of the meat in whatever form they like it. For Henry, the shape of the meat had to resemble a chicken breast. Place the tiniest bite of one of the vegetables on a separate plate and, in a matter-of-fact way, make it clear that it is to be eaten. That's your starting point:

every time you serve that dish, repeat this pattern, upping the vegetables little by little.

Kicking back

A home lunch is probably the only meal we eat when we are not on a schedule. No one needs to be ready for school; the meal isn't squeezed between acres of homework, downtime and an early bedtime. Home lunches are just that little bit more relaxed.

For days when Henry's home on school vacations and weekends, lunches are great. I tend to cook something nourishing and easy with minimum clearing up. (There are only so many times I am prepared to pack and unpack that dreaded dishwasher.) Lunches at home are also the perfect time to get Henry involved in food preparation. Henry loves to cook and his punctilious nature means that recipes are followed to the letter and turn out fantastically well – as opposed to my slapdash methods, which are usually dictated by time and patience constraints and what I can only describe as an allergic reaction to written instruction. A winning scenario that works is when Henry bakes a cake for dessert while I coax the main course into being. We make a great team: Henry is commis chef to my chef de partie. Here are a few double-duty lunches where the objective, apart from midday nourishment, is to empower my son and give him the opportunity to explore foods and understand their qualities before he's asked to consume them.

Pork with apples and cabbage (Me)

followed by

wholewheat chocolate bloomer (Henry)

PORK WITH APPLES AND CABBAGE

This has the advantage of being cooked together but served separately if required – and there's only one pan to wash! The secret to achieving soft, even-textured meat is to sear it properly to keep the meat moist and be careful not to overcook it. A pork tenderloin is a long, thin piece of meat that should cook through in 20 minutes.

ingredients

- 2 pork tenderloins
- Vegetable oil for the pan (e.g. sunflower or canola/rapeseed oil)
- 8oz (250g) streaky bacon, cut into short strips
- Small cabbage, roughly chopped
- 2 eating apples, cored and sliced
- ½ pint (150ml) vegetable stock (see recipe on page 63)

Method

Preheat the oven to 425°F/220°C/200°C fan/gas mark 7.

Start by trimming the tenderloins, taking off any membrane or coating around the meat as it can be stringy when cooked. Then take a large stove-to-oven casserole dish, add a tablespoon of oil and heat for a couple of minutes before adding the bacon. Fry the bacon until well done, by which time a good deal of the fat will have come out into the pan. Spoon out the bacon on to a plate and, with the oil good and hot, spend 10 minutes browning the pork tenderloins, making sure they are properly seared, sealing in all the juices. Turn off the heat and take the tenderloins out of the casserole and set to one side. Arrange the cabbage, bacon and apple along the bottom of the casserole, pour over the stock, then sit the tenderloins on top. Put the lid on and place the casserole dish in the oven for 20 minutes. The pork will be cooked through, but the cabbage and apple won't have turned to mush and should still be nicely intact.

The pork can be sliced and served with neat piles of bacon, cabbage and apple in separate places on the plate, although Henry invariably leaves the apple because it has soaked up the pork flavours and 'doesn't taste right'.

WHOLEWHEAT CHOCOLATE BLOOMER

This is a fantastic low-sugar dessert. I'll admit this is pandering to what Henry best loves to eat in all the world, but it is satisfying from a deep pressure sensory perspective when he kneads the bread and does it for his taste buds at the same time. I could add 'mixing textures' to the benefits of this dish, but that would be lame because add bread or chocolate to just about anything and he'll eat it.

We always try to make enough for breakfast the next morning but we haven't managed that yet. If we time it so that Henry is kneading the dough for the second time as I am starting preparation of the pork, then it usually works out that the bread is cooking while we are eating the main course and comes out just at the right time ready for devouring!

ingredients

- ¼oz (7g/1 sachet) dried yeast
- ½ tbsp honey or agave syrup
- 1¼ cups (300ml) tepid water
- 4 cups (500g) wholewheat bread flour or half wholewheat/half white bread flour
- 2 tsp salt
- 1½ cups (200g) of your favourite chocolate, broken into small chunks
- ¼ cup (50ml) milk

Method

Dissolve the yeast, honey or agave and half the water in a cup or small bowl and leave for 10 minutes until it is frothy and has doubled in volume. Then put the flour and salt into a large bowl and stir in the yeast mixture with a fork, gradually adding the remainder of the water. When you have a nice dough, transfer to a floured surface and knead it for at least 10 minutes by pushing the dough in with your fist and folding it back on itself, squashing it down with your knuckles. Do this in different directions over and over, and then transfer the dough to a clean, floured bowl. Cover it with Saran Wrap/cling film or put a damp tea towel over the top and put it somewhere warm to rise for about an hour.

In the meantime, grease and flour a large baking tray. When the dough has doubled in size, scrape it out of the bowl on to a floured surface and bash all the air out of it and knead it for another 5 minutes. The next step is to get the chocolate in there and how you do that is really up to you! We make the dough into a flattened rugby ball and then use a pastry brush to paint a thick line of milk about 1" (2cm) in from the top and put chocolate chunks along that line. Roll the dough from the pointy end over the chocolate, paste the next line with milk, add chocolate and roll over again. Just keep doing this until you have packed your dough with chocolate. The tricky bit is getting the end bit to stick, but a liberal daubing of milk should work.

Place the dough on the baking tray with the last seam at the bottom to hold it and put the tray in a warm place for 10–15 minutes to prove. Set your oven to 325°F/160°C/140°C fan/gas mark 3. Then bake your bloomer on the middle shelf for about 50 minutes. It is cooked when you tap it on the bottom and it makes a hollow sound. Henry loves to pull this apart before devouring and we all love it smothered in butter.

Salmon with mixed vegetables
and bread and butter
(Me: frying the salmon; Henry: veg prep)

followed by

Flapjack (Henry)

Henry starts off by making the flapjack because the main course cooks very quickly.

FLAPJACK

I tried to keep the sugar as low as possible in this recipe: a bit of a challenge as the binding agent and the chewy texture in flapjacks usually comes from a hefty input of syrup. Here it is a token gesture to achieve that texture. Honey is a wonderful substitute because you can get away with using less of it as it has a much sweeter taste. The peanut butter adds protein as well as cementing everything together, and the apple also adds sweetness. Chewy has become Henry's texture of choice; a good way to get him to try new foods is to achieve that desired chewiness and then add new flavours. With this flapjack, try switching out the peanut butter for other butters such as almond, macadamia or tahini.

ingredients

- 1 stick (100g) butter
- 1 tbsp smooth peanut butter
- 1 tbsp honey
- 1 tbsp syrup (agave, rice or golden)
- 2 apples, peeled and finely grated
- 2½ cups (250g) rolled oats
- Small pinch salt

Method

Butter an 8" (20cm) square tin and set the oven at 325°F/160°C/140°C fan/gas mark 3. Using a thick-bottomed pan over a medium heat, start by adding the butter, peanut butter, honey and syrup and cook until the mixture boils. Then turn off the heat and add the apple, oats and salt. Stir together thoroughly. Spoon the mixture into the buttered tin, pressing it down with the back of a clean dessert spoon so the flapjack mixture is tightly packed and smoothed off. Bake for about 40 minutes on the middle shelf until golden brown. Leave to cool in the tin and score the pieces while it's still quite hot. Ours usually gets eaten straight from the tin!

SALMON WITH MIXED VEGETABLES AND BREAD AND BUTTER

ingredients (serves 4)

- 4 salmon steaks
- Carrots, kale, beans, broccoli – whatever vegetables are good and in season
- Fresh bread and butter
- Olive oil to fry

Method

Once the flapjack is in the oven, I get on with frying the salmon and Henry prepares the vegetables. Before cooking the fish, check for bones – always a good idea even if they are fillets. Just run your fingers firmly along the sides and top of the fish. You should see layers of paler and darker flesh in the raw fillet, and it's where those layers meet that you may find bones. Anything hard and spiky, get in there and pull it out. Use tweezers if you have to. Next, heat a solid frying pan with a liberal covering of olive oil. When the oil starts smoking, add the fish skin-side down. I like to cook the skin fast and get it really crispy; that way the centre of the salmon stays succulent. Be careful not to overcook salmon as it quickly goes dry. Depending on the size of your fillet, fry the skin side for 5–10 minutes and then flip over and fry the other side. Henry doesn't eat the skin but there are plenty of us around the table who will!

Meanwhile, Henry is prepping the vegetables and placing them in the steamer. The steamer has three levels and it is interesting to discuss how size and density affects the cooking time of each vegetable. Carrots usually go on first and a leaf vegetable such as kale literally only takes a couple of minutes. Lightly steamed and al dente, these vegetables come to the plate with their vitamins intact.

Simply fried salmon is absolutely delicious; just add steamed vegetables and bread and butter for the perfect easy, nutritious lunch. And the flapjack should be cooling through the main course all ready for dessert.

Burgers
(Henry: Burgers and fixings;
Me: Help with the fixings)

followed by

Steamed sponge (Me)

BURGERS

Up until age nine Henry ate his burgers in their constituent parts. At nine, however, he felt he could bite meat plus bun and now we are working on introducing the fixings, which start on the side of the plate and then graduate to inside the bun.

The key to a great burger, of course, is to use the very best-quality meat. Opt for ground beef steak or turkey.

We also like ground buffalo meat, which has a lighter, sweeter flavour and, according to the pack, has twice the protein of beef and is higher in iron and all the omegas. Buffalo meat also has 70–90 per cent less fat than beef, but we don't care about that. We like fat. The British have been slow to catch on to buffalo meat, so I always scan the meat section in the supermarket for bargains when the buffalo packs are close to their sell-by date and marked down.

I probably had the most disposable income I have ever had in my teens because I held down two or three jobs simultaneously, usually in kitchens. At 14, I was sweating out my weekends over a giant griddle flipping burgers in a road-side cafe. Now that 'flipping' knowledge I am passing on to my children. What I really want to impart to them is that there is nothing like a double shift, earning minimum wage, at a hot, stinking griddle to urge you to go that extra mile at school to pump up your grades, giving you other future earning options.

ingredients (serves 4)

- 3 tbsp all-purpose flour
- 1lb (500g) top-quality ground beef/turkey/buffalo meat
- 1 egg yolk
- Pinch salt
- Olive oil for frying
- 4 white bread buns

Method

These burgers are, of course, without onions and herbs. Neurotypicals can add all those extra perks later when they customize their own meal.

Cover your counter or a board with flour. Mix the ground meat, egg yolk and a pinch of salt in a large bowl with fingers or a fork. Divide the meat mixture into four, roll it into balls in your palms and then flatten to make patties. Cover each patty in flour, lay them out on a tray and place in the fridge for 20–30 minutes.

The burgers are more likely to stay intact in the frying pan if first chilled. Meanwhile, set about preparing the fixings.

Fixings

- Sliced red onions
- Sliced chilli
- Sweet chilli sauce
- Lettuce
- Sliced cheese
- Bacon, cooked to your liking
- Sliced tomatoes, cucumber, gherkin
- Spicy tomato chutney

The fixings, to use the American parlance, are, of course, for the benefit of other family members who crave variety and actually love mixing tastes and textures. This approach to a meal also works very well in reverse for hyposensitive Aspergers whose preference is for stronger or spicier flavours, providing tailor-made fixings for a bland meal that needs extra kick.

Henry is very happy making the burgers and we share the preparation of the fixings. Even though he wouldn't eat most of what is on the list above, preparing these off-limits foods familiarizes him with their smells and characteristics. Exposure to new foods, I believe, helps break established food habits. Lettuce, for instance, thought to be utterly revolting, has been on the table and occasionally prepared by Henry for years. But this year lettuce made it into the bun along with the bacon. Onion and tomato are still some way off.

Cooking the burgers

When the patties are sufficiently chilled, heat a heavy-bottomed pan over a high flame, add a healthy slug of olive oil (yes, I know olive oil loses all its goodness at high temperature, but I like the taste) and place in your patties, cooking each side for about 5 minutes. Put the bread buns cut side up under the grill until they are lightly toasted. This adds another nice texture layer to your burger but also prevents the burger making the bread soggy. I send all the constituent parts out separately so everyone can make up their plate as they wish.

STEAMED SPONGE

I throw the sponge together as Henry is getting the counter laid out with all he needs to make the burgers. So for almost all our burger and fixing prep time this lovely pudding is sitting on the back of the stove bubbling away. As per usual I have done my best to reduce the sugar by adding a sweet-tasting rogue element, prunes, which also add fabulous amounts of fibre. Traditionally for this kind of pudding you would spoon generous amounts of jam or chocolate sauce or fruit such as chopped apple or pineapple into the bowl before adding the mixture and steaming, to give the sponge a lovely gooey topping. Feel free to do this if your child likes it this way. We prefer ours plain.

ingredients

- 1 cup (150g) prunes
- ¾ cup (200ml) boiling water
- 1½ sticks (150g) butter, melted, and extra butter for greasing
- ½ cup (50g) sugar
- 3 eggs, whisked
- 2 cups wholewheat flour + 2 tsp baking powder (200g wholemeal self-raising flour)

Method

Put the prunes in a bowl with the water and allow to sit for an hour. Drain off the excess water and blend to a mush.

Liberally grease a 2 pint (1 litre) pudding basin with butter. In a large bowl cream the melted butter and sugar, mix in the prunes and the eggs, and then fold in the flour. Beat the mixture thoroughly with a wooden spoon, then spoon it into the basin. Take a sheet of greaseproof paper and smear butter over an area large enough to cover the top of the basin. Fold a pleat into the paper to allow for expansion and, allowing the folded paper paper to sit loosely above the pudding mixture, butter side down, secure it with string around the lip of the bowl and then cut off the excess paper. Put the basin in a large pan and fill halfway up the side of the basin with water. Bring the water to a steady simmer, put the lid on the pan and let it cook away gently for about 1½ hours, when a skewer inserted in the centre of the pudding should come out clean. Check every half-hour or so in case the water needs topping up.

Be careful of the super-heated steam when you take the bowl out of the pan. Run a palette knife round the pudding and turn it out on to a serving dish. I like to serve this with crème fraîche. My husband wishes I would make custard. I am not a custard fan but occasionally I indulge him!

Skills for life

Home cooking with Mum or Dad is a perfect place for a child, whether ASD or not, to learn how to handle hot pans and sharp knives. In this age where children aren't allowed to handle anything sharper than a golf ball, I fear for their safety. That sounds like a contradiction, but it isn't. Handling sharp and potentially harmful objects with an adult a few feet away is vital developmental know-how. Only hands-on experience is any good, in my opinion. In the kitchen choose a process that's age-appropriate – in other words, don't let your six-year-old deep-fat-fry, but do let them cut up the vegetables, boil the kettle, open the hot oven door. Instruct and watch from a distance; just don't do it for them and they'll learn.

An unexpected lunch happening (as a comic aside)

We have had some odd meals over the years. Such as the time, when touring Europe, we hit Belgium on a national holiday and had to share two dried croissants between the four of us because even the service stations were out of food. Or a day out at the Chicago Zoo when the cocoa flask leaked on to the sandwiches and we were forced to consume soggy chocolatey ham, bread and butter mush. I never like to throw food away if it is at all edible.

These lunches hardly count when compared with the day we ate road kill. It stemmed from the constant nagging inflicted by Henry's younger brother, Will, about the awful waste of good food that lay about, freshly slaughtered, on the narrow lanes that criss-cross the countryside in our bit of Kent, particularly rabbit and pheasant. I have always made it clear to my children that eating a good diet is a privilege most people round the globe are sadly unable to enjoy, and this perhaps sparked Will's zealous enthusiasm for free and ready fare. But whenever we were out and about in the car and Will tried to persuade me to stop and pick up something freshly murdered by the road, I always made my excuses, usually that there wasn't a safe place to pull over or it looked unfit for consumption.

Early one Saturday morning, though, Will was being driven by his dad to football practice and a quarter of a mile from our house he spotted a freshly dead pheasant. I got a very excited phone call from the car asking me to pick it up, followed by another urgent call to 'run now' because Will had spotted a neighbour walking the other way who was, he felt, sure to nab the bird if he got to it first. Honestly, the things you do for your children. So I dashed up the lane in my dressing gown and wellies, feeling a complete fool, and retrieved the dead bird which was surprisingly intact, if not a little crushed on one side. Back home, Henry came down into the kitchen to see what I was up to and I wasn't quite sure what his reaction would be to this limp feathered object in my hand that was destined to be lunch.

Meat we buy in the supermarket is so overly packaged – presented as neat pieces cellophane-wrapped on a polystyrene tray – that it bears little resemblance to the animal it came from. I actually thought that this was a good exercise for the boys to connect the once-living bird with a meal on the table. So I tried to be as matter-of-fact about it as I could and laid the pheasant out on a roasting tray (it was dripping a bit) and put it on the worktop ready for inspection. Henry was at once fascinated and upset. Remarkably, he was distressed not for the sad demise of this pretty bird but for the lovely lunch we were denying the local fox community! When he had got over that, he spent an age closely inspecting the bird's impressive plumage with its fabulous iridescence. When Will got home from football, the boys plucked the pheasant, taking no notice of my pleas to do it gently, and the slightly mauled result, after we had gutted it, was shoved into a casserole dish with stock and veggies. It actually had a fantastic flavour and Henry happily ate the meat, refusing the vegetables, of course. That was a real highlight in our new wave of culinary exploration, definitely not one to be forgotten.

Sunday Lunches (that can just as easily happen on a Saturday)

GLAZED HAM

If not too salty and certainly not smoked, a lovely thick piece of ham is now vying with chicken for top place on Henry's meats-to-eat list. Initially introduced as ham slices in his lunch box, bland, tasteless sandwich ham was so close in flavour and texture to chicken that it was readily accepted, aged eight. At age nine, Henry progressed to the home-cooked variety.

I do like to boil a ham in an acidic, sweet or fruity liquor as this tenderizes and sweetens the meat. I tried Nigella's ham cooked in coke, which works well, but the slight coke taste left in the meat didn't go down well with my Aspie. Some other boiling options are red wine, orangeade, dandelion and burdock, ginger beer – the list is almost endless, depending on how traditional or trashy you want to go. Apple cider (the British alcoholic variety) is my favourite, closely followed by good old-fashioned vegetable stock.

At first glance, some of the ingredients below won't seem to be Asperger friendly and that's because they are not. But they do only appear on three-quarters of the ham, cordoned off by the peppercorns. Many recipes also use mustard powder, but I can't abide the taste, so I use the fresher variety and the whole mustard seeds give the ham fantastic extra zing.

ingredients (serves 4)

- 4½–6½lb (2–3kg) cured uncooked ham (essentially a large hunk of bacon), on the bone
- 2–3 pints (1–2 litres) cider, dry or sweet depending on your preference
- ½ cup (100g) dark brown sugar
- Peppercorns
- Wholegrain mustard
- Cloves

Method

To reduce the saltiness of the ham, either soak it in cold water overnight or boil it for half an hour and drain off the water before returning the meat to the pan. The water used for soaking or boiling should be saved as it makes a super base for a stock. Personally, I prefer the soaking method.

In the pan, cover the ham, skin intact, with cider. Obviously, the bigger the pan, the more cider you will need to cover the meat but the cooking will require less scrutiny as the pan's unlikely to boil dry. Cook on the stove top for 30 minutes for every 1lb (500g). So for a 5lb (2½kg) ham, that's 2½ hours. Skim off any fat that floats to the surface and top up the cider to keep the ham covered.

When the cooking time is almost up, set the oven to 400°F/200°C/180°C fan/gas mark 6. The ham is ready when a fork inserted into the meat goes in and comes out easily. Then remove the ham from the pan and set it on a roasting tray. Cut the skin off, leaving a layer of the fat underneath maybe ⅛" (3mm) thick.

Score the fat, taking care not to cut into the meat, in a criss-cross pattern, making diamond shapes all over the skin. Cover the whole area of fat with the brown sugar. Then I designate a quarter to be just sugar glaze and cordon it off using the peppercorns. Cover the remaining three-quarters of the fatty area with wholegrain mustard and then another layer of sugar on top of that. Push the cloves into the points of the diamond pattern on the mustard side. Then place the ham on a roasting tray and put it into the oven to glaze for 30 minutes.

I serve this ham with any vegetables that will get a favourable reception and mashed potatoes. Up until about a year ago Henry didn't like the mashed texture and would only eat evenly cut boiled potatoes that I whipped out of the pan and set to one side before proceeding to mash the rest.

ROAST DUCK

Duck makes for a wonderful special lunch and it goes down so well with all the family. I often cook two at once to ensure enough meat for subsequent lunches and other dishes. Henry adores the breast meat because it is really just a 'special kind of chicken'.

In my efforts to get him to accept gravies and sauces, and because the rest of us love it, I make a gravy that is fully flavoursome and pretty rich, but in my opinion there is really no other gravy that will do for a duck. Henry will now tolerate the smallest dot of this gravy on the very edge of his plate. He's actually been allowed to ignore it until about three months ago, when he decided he could take a tiny dab of it on his fork and taste it. I suspect this level of consumption will go on for a very long time until he accepts more of it; eventually, I hope he puts it on his duck and eats the two together.

ingredients

- 4½lb (2kg) duck (with giblets)
- 1 stick celery
- 1 carrot
- 1 onion
- Knob of butter
- Bay leaf
- Glass of red wine (optional)
- Salt
- Redcurrant jelly (optional)

Gravy

Make sure you buy a duck with its giblets and then the first job is to make the gravy. Roughly chop a stick of celery, a carrot and an onion plus the giblets and fry them all in a pan with a knob of butter. Fry for about 10 minutes until the meat is brown and the vegetables are beginning to caramelize. Next add 2 cups (500ml) of water and a bay leaf, and gently simmer for a little over an hour. Feel free to pour in a glass of red wine (as I know you are drinking it anyway), just to add another dimension to the sauce. While the gravy is simmering, you can get on with the main job in hand and that's to cook the duck.

The duck

A top tip I learnt many years ago from a Delia Smith cookery book was to dry the duck's skin thoroughly before cooking. So as soon as I have bought it, the uncooked bird gets a good blotting with paper towel and then sits in the fridge without its wrapping for a day or so to thoroughly dry out. This means that the skin goes beautifully crispy when cooked. Thank you, Delia.

Method

Preheat the oven to 425°F/220°C/200°C fan/gas mark 7. Take a metal skewer and pierce the duck skin all over. This allows the fat to run out of the bird, which pretty much self-bastes as it cooks. I rub salt but not pepper into the skin, place the duck on a rack in a roasting pan and put it on the middle shelf of the oven. Give the duck half an hour per 1lb (500g) plus an extra 20 minutes for luck. Baste the duck once or twice and then drain the fat off from the tray and set it aside in a basin to cool as it produces absolutely perfect roast potatoes. Removing this fat also cuts down the spattering to the oven. There is no doubt that cooking duck does make an almighty mess of your oven and you can choose to cover the bird with foil for all or part of the cooking time. But the duck is in no danger of drying out, and if you want that delicious crispy skin, you are just going to have to break out the scouring pad and Marigolds.

The last duck I cooked was 3½lb (1.6kg) and it was ready in almost exactly 2 hours. The gravy needs about that amount of time, so the duck and gravy should be ready roughly at the same point. And during that cooking time you'll have no doubt rustled up some wonderful veggies. Move the duck from the roasting pan to a serving dish, draining out any juices trapped in the bird's cavity, and leave to rest for 20 minutes as this will tenderize the meat. Carefully pour off the fat in the roasting pan and add it to the other fat. Add the juices left in the bottom of the pan to the gravy. Next sieve the gravy to remove the giblets and vegetables and boil rapidly for 10 minutes to thicken it, adding a tablespoon of cornstarch if needs be, and serve. You could also sweeten the gravy with a teaspoon or two of redcurrant jelly.

MEAT LOAF

This is a great recipe to make use of meat left over from a roast. Here I am combining chicken and ham, but duck, beef and venison also work very well. This is also a natural progression for your child from eating a plain piece of meat to a meaty dish that tastes almost exactly the same but, rather as the meatballs do, challenges their notion of what meat can look like. Meat doesn't have to be a uniform and recognized size and shape. Taking it a step further still, try adding chunks of an already favoured food such as carrot or apple as an extended texture challenge!

ingredients

- Butter for greasing
- 1 cup (200ml) hot milk
- 4oz (100g) bread, crusts cut off, pulled into small bits
- 1lb (500g) cooked chicken and ham
- 2 eggs, beaten
- Pinch salt

Method

Butter a 2lb (900g) loaf tin. Preheat the oven to 375°F/190°C/ 170°C fan/gas mark 5. Heat the milk to boiling point in a pan and add the bread. Either finely chop the meat by hand or use a food processor. Then add the milky bready mix to the food processor or use a fork to combine it with the meat. Beat the eggs in a bowl and mix thoroughly with the chicken, bread mixture and a pinch of salt. To change the texture and make this loaf less spongy, you can use crackers instead of bread and not chop the meat so finely, leaving it a little chunky. Pack the mixture down into the buttered loaf tin and bake for about an hour. Allow the loaf to cool before turning out on to a board to slice.

Sick boy lunches

The emotional energy required just to get through an average day is utterly draining for an Asperger. Some mornings it is clear that Henry's not feeling particularly robust. That is to say, not physically ailing but emotionally 'under the weather'. So we take the executive decision to sit back and regroup, and hope to come up smiling the next day. These quiet, delicate days call for soothing sustenance.

MARROW DUMPLINGS

Marrow is definitely underused in our modern diet. It is full of protein and makes a super smooth base for soups, stews and dumplings. Marrow dumplings are an old recipe and many countries have their own version with chopped herbs, nutmeg, lemon rind and ground beef or chicken. But mine are very plain and uniform with no bits. Ask your butcher to cut the marrowbone into short sections. After half an hour at room temperature you are able to scoop out the nutritious fatty marrow into a bowl that can then chill in the fridge.

ingredients

- 7oz (200g) white spongy bread, pulled into rough breadcrumbs (brioche is best as it's springy and produces lovely light dumplings)
- 1¼ cups (300ml) whole milk
- 5 cups (1½ litres) chicken stock (see page 63)
- 7oz (200g) chilled beef marrow
- 3 eggs, lightly whisked
- 1 tsp salt

Method

Place the breadcrumbs in a medium bowl and pour over the milk. Squish the bread and milk together with your fingers and leave to soak for 15 minutes. Pour the chicken stock into a medium pan to a depth of about 2" (4cm) and bring slowly to a simmer. Meanwhile place your beef marrow into a large bowl. Bring the milky breadcrumbs over by the marrow bowl. Take handfuls of breadcrumbs and squeeze the milk out before adding to the marrow. Use a wooden spoon to blend the marrow thoroughly with the milky breadcrumbs, then add the eggs and salt. If the mixture is sloppy, add a little all-purpose flour to firm it up before placing the bowl back in the fridge for 10 minutes; it is easier to form the dumplings with a chilled mixture.

Use this time to tidy up and check on your stock. It should be nicely simmering. Take the dumpling mix out of the fridge and, using a heaped teaspoon at a time, roll the mixture into balls. I like to make small ones about 1" (2cm) diameter because they cook quickly and cool quickly, but you can make them any size. For bigger dumplings, cook only a couple at a time so the broth doesn't lose heat; otherwise, they get soggy. Pop four or five small dumplings into the bubbling broth and in about 5 minutes, depending on their size, they should all float, which means they are done. Scoop out the dumplings with a slotted spoon and serve. The meaty goodness of the marrow, together with the eggs and the absorbed chicken broth, makes a marvellous dish for a child in need of fortification.

Being so fluffy and light, these dumplings come across as something close to chicken-flavoured bread. They are easy to eat and digest, while ticking the pale, even-textured and bready boxes. Switch the chicken broth for beef if that's preferred. Don't waste the leftover stock; use it for rice or noodles later. In the interests of food hygiene, however, I would chill it and then bring it to a healthy boil before recycling it, and use it that day if possible.

CORN AND CHICKEN BAKE

Here we have another combination of a favoured texture and flavour. What you get here is a sort of chicken cake. Both elements are winners with Henry, and in the past I have added a smidge of honey if I felt it was needed to make it even more appealing. Bizarre, but it goes down very well.

ingredients

- Butter for greasing
- 1 cup (150g) cornmeal or polenta soaked in 1 cup (300ml) just-boiled chicken stock for 20 minutes
- 1 tbsp cornstarch
- 3 large eggs
- 4 tbsp melted butter
- ⅔ cup (150ml) whole milk
- 1lb (500g) boiled chicken, finely shredded

Method

Set the oven at 350°F/180°C/160°C fan/gas mark 4 and butter a medium casserole dish. Mix all the ingredients together in a large bowl and then turn out into the casserole dish. Bake on the middle shelf for about 30 minutes until a skewer inserted in the centre comes out clean. Leave to cool in the casserole dish and then serve in slices.

MILK TOAST

This is such an old recipe: simple, soothing and nourishing. Henry doesn't like his too soggy so I hold back with the milk. I also add powdered vitamins, formulated especially for children, which can be bought from good health food stores. Although I don't advocate using vitamins on a regular basis because I think that children should get their nutrients from food, a vitamin boost when a child is off-colour can make all the difference.

ingredients

- ½ cup (100ml) milk
- 1 tsp all-purpose flour
- ⅔ cup (150ml) light (single) cream
- A knob of butter
- A doorstep (very thick slice) of day-old white bread
- 1 tsp brown sugar, agave, maple syrup or honey
- Children's vitamin powder

Method

Add half of the milk to a pan on a low heat and warm gently. Add the flour, stirring with a wooden spoon. Once the flour and milk are blended together, slowly add the rest of the milk, cream and butter. Bring to the boil, stirring continuously, and then turn off the heat and allow to stand for a minute or two. When it has cooled to something close to body temperature add the vitamins (the appropriate amount for 1 cup (250ml) of liquid, as stated on the pack) and stir in thoroughly. Meanwhile, toast the bread and cut off the crusts. Place the toast in a shallow bowl, pour over the warm milky mixture, removing any skin that may have formed, stopping when the toast has reached its maximum soaking point. Cover the toast with a sprinkling of brown sugar, agave, maple syrup or honey. I usually chop it into squares for ease of forking.

RICE CAKE

This is a rather bland, gluten-free, comforting cake made with rice flour and a little honey. It is a safe and easy option when feeding your Asperger is a challenge. The eggs and ground almonds provide a nice amount of protein, and this cake makes a great accompaniment to eggs, peanut butter, ham slices or anything you can think of.

ingredients

- 1 stick (100g) butter and extra for greasing
- 2 tbsp honey
- 3 eggs
- 2 cups (200g) rice flour
- 1½ cups (200g) ground almonds
- 3 tsp baking powder (gluten-free)
- 3 tbsp single cream

Method

Preheat the oven to 350°F/180°C/160°C fan/gas mark 4. Grease and line a loaf tin with baking paper or, if like me you can't stand to faff around with baking paper, use an ovenproof loaf-shaped Pyrex dish which works just as well and is quicker and easier to clean.

Cream the butter and the honey together and then beat in the eggs. Next, fold in the rice four, ground almonds and baking powder. Then gently mix in the cream. Feel free to add another spoonful of milk if the mixture is too cloying. It should have the consistency of fine wet sand! Spoon the mixture into your loaf tin and bake in the centre of the oven for about 40 minutes or until a skewer inserted into the centre of the cake comes out clean. Cool on a wire rack.

Getting better at lunches is the key to cracking dinners. Lunches are much less pressured, whereas at dinnertime, certainly in our house, it's all going on and everyone is that little bit more tired after a busy day. For that reason, lunches should really get a lot easier, with a bigger variety of food eaten, before dinners do. And particularly if you have a child under seven, make your special celebratory meals at lunchtime. I guarantee *everyone* will be on better form.

chapter 5

Snacks and Drinks

When Henry has eaten very little at a meal – maybe because he didn't like it or was just feeling out of sorts – then I am faced with the dilemma of persisting with the current meal, which can be a long and protracted process, or giving up and getting him through to the next scheduled mealtime via a snack. The latter has been our best strategy, but it only works if the snacks are small. Otherwise, we enter a mad chicken-and-egg scenario in which my well-snacked child isn't hungry for a full-sized meal and then doesn't eat sufficient food to sustain him through to the next meal and so craves another large snack! So be wary of setting your child up to be a serial snacker. Fix mealtimes, fix snack times and limit the size of snacks to about 200 calories, which is roughly one slice of wholewheat toast with a tablespoon of almond butter or two wheat crackers and a hard-boiled egg.

The concept of three meals a day and two light nibbles has always been a bit of a battleground between us because Henry has an innate tendency to snack. He prefers ad hoc grazing over set meals because snacks are small bites eaten casually, demanding very little social interaction and not an awful lot of sitting down. Compared with meals, snacks are simple and no stress.

Fitting in a snack between meals avoids the dreaded mid-afternoon energy slump characterized by listlessness and lack of concentration. And, of course, choosing to eat slow-burning snack foods prevents the rapid highs and severe sugar lows that my Aspie has a particularly hard time dealing with.

It is really important to leave a sensible gap between meals and snacks; my rule is no more than four hours and no less than two. This allows food to be digested properly between eating and also gets your child accustomed to one of the most basic of sensations: feeling full and feeling empty, and getting up a healthy appetite for the next meal. These primal connections with the body are part of the natural rhythm of the day and, I think, vitally important for a child with Asperger's. A constant state of half-full isn't good for digestion or general wellbeing, and actually that's what over-snacking creates.

Snack choice

What to give as a snack? Like all children, Henry loves, loves, loves sugar. A sweet cereal such as Cheerios would probably feature at the top of his favourite foods. But sugar has a horrible effect on his behaviour, making him hyper, followed by a depressive slump. So we aim to opt for a savoury or very-low-sugar snack. This is a tough one in a world where traditional nibbles are packed with sugar. Even granola bars, energy drinks and smoothies that claim to be healthy are laden with it. Look for sugar on the ingredients list of any packet food. Don't be fooled by the pseudonyms either. Anything with an 'ose' is sugar – including maltose, lactose, fructose, glucose and sucrose. It has no nutritional value, completely messes up the metabolism and, according to Dr Lustig,[1] a paediatrician who specializes in overweight children, it is sugar and its effect on the body's insulin that makes children fat. Furthermore, a study by Professor Joseph Schroeder,[2] director of behavioural neuroscience at Connecticut College, showed sugar to be more addictive than one of the most powerful psychoactive

1   R. H. Lustig (2013) *Fat Chance: Beating the Odds Against Sugar, Processed Food, Obesity, and Disease.* New York: Hudson Street Press.

2   *Connecticut College News* (2013) 'Student-faculty research suggests Oreos can be compared to drugs of abuse in lab rats.' Available at www.conncoll.edu/news/news-archive/2013/student-faculty-research-suggests-oreos-can-be-compared-to-drugs-of-abuse-in-lab-rats.htm#.VAsjD1ZKdHg, accessed on 18 September 2014.

chemicals known to man – cocaine. Given the choice of sugar or cocaine, rats went for the sweet stuff! You can see this played out in any supermarket: just watch a mum try to pay for her groceries with a young child in tow who is begging and pleading for the treats and sweets sitting tantalizingly by the till.

Before I began to scrutinize Henry's diet, I hadn't realized just how much sugar in all its forms we consumed as a family. Two of the biggest culprits were fruit juice – even though it is fructose (fruit sugar), it's still just *sugar* with all the associated downsides – and yoghurts which hide up to a whopping five teaspoons of sugar in every small 5oz (150g) healthy-looking pot. What's more, sugar seems to have snuck into almost everything. Why, for instance, is it in salad dressing, and why is there so much of it in barbecue sauce? Foods that should be savoury, such as fish fingers and pasta sauce, also contain sugar, presumably to make them more palatable. But even these savoury foods actually only contain a tiny amount of sugar compared to the heaps and heaps of it in cookies, sweets and sodas that deliver a sugar hit that's akin to a large blow to the back of the head.

Once I was convinced of the negative effect of sugar on Henry's constitution, I became fairly militant about what he was and wasn't allowed to eat when he was away from my care. Some well-meaning friends and relatives thought that I was making too much of the sugar issue and as a fully paid-up food fanatic was denying my son some of the greatest joys central to childhood – namely the stuffing in of sweets, candies and cookies as 'treats' for that feeling of happy, buzzy contentment.

A boy's ninth birthday party sticks in my mind as a particularly low (and I mean that both ways) sugar moment. At drop-off I had a quiet word with the party host, my son's friend's mother, about the fact that Henry knows he shouldn't eat sugar and he's fine with that, so please don't offer it to him. Three hours later the same lady opened the door to me and I could tell from the expression on her face that things were not going well. I dragged a manic, crazed Henry out of their garden and into the car. He'd been given six chocolate cookies.

'He just really loved them and all the other kids were having some. I felt bad that he was being left out,' she said.

'But SIX!'

'He just kept eating them. He really liked them.'

'Yes, I suppose he did really like them. Did you offer him a cigarette as well? Maybe a line of cocaine?' I thought as I tried to restrain a hysterical boy who was laughing like a madman and kicking out in all directions. Something I felt I would also do if I didn't leave promptly.

Buckling Henry into the car was like containing an exploding firework, his arms flailing about and so silly I had trouble closing the door for fear that he'd lash out at the last minute and lose a finger. As we eventually made our exit, I switched on the CD player and turned up Henry's favourite audio book of Hugh Bonneville reading Gerald Durrell's *My Family and Other Animals*, to get him to focus and quieten, and also so he couldn't hear the string of expletives I was mumbling as we drove back home. Half an hour later, I had a weeping, depressed child with fingers twitching and hands shaking: something he does when he's extremely unhappy and out of sorts. It took two days for normality to be resumed. Lesson learnt.

As Henry gets older, it does get easier because he's more in tune with the effect foods have on him; he understands his body's responses to things like sugar and so he's better at avoiding them. But what nine-year-old can refuse a chocolate cookie at a party? Maybe that really is asking too much.

Snacks that work for us

To my mind, the perfect snack should be a combination of carbohydrate, fat and protein: in essence, a mini meal. This is our current snack list to be mixed and matched.

Single-texture raw fruit and veg

Always, always, always I am trying to up Henry's daily quota of fresh fruit and vegetables and I do worry that there's still a great deal of repetition here. Put it this way, I buy a 2lb (1kg) bag of carrots and broccoli and 4lb (2kg) of apples every week! But little bites of whatever else he will eat beyond his core favourites – French beans, melon, raisins, bananas and de-skinned oranges – all go a long way to upping that quota.

Low-sugar breads and muffins

Here I am again with the bready equivalents. Combined with a slice of ham or peanut butter and a carrot stick, though, they're a perfect mid-morning or mid-afternoon snack. Here are some we really like.

WELSH CAKES

These are delicious fried cakes. You must use lard – nothing else will do! A Welsh cake is a pretty substantial beast, invented, I expect, to sustain sheep farmers out on cold wet hillsides or to invigorate hardworking coal miners. Welsh cakes work equally well for Aspergers in need of proper sustenance.

ingredients

- 2 cups (225g) all-purpose flour
- ¼ cup (50g) superfine sugar
- 1 tsp baking powder
- Pinch salt
- Small pinch mixed spice (pinch is hardly detectable – build up to 2 tsp)
- ½ stick (50g) butter, cut into small pieces
- 2oz (50g) lard, cut into small pieces
- 1 egg, beaten
- 4 tbsp milk
- Extra lard for frying

Method

Mix the flour, sugar, baking powder, salt and mixed spice together in a large bowl. Welsh cakes aren't really Welsh cakes without mixed spice, but if your child won't tolerate even the tiniest hint of this flavour, please omit it. Add the butter and lard, and rub in with your fingers until the mixture resembles breadcrumbs. Then mix in the beaten egg and milk with a fork until you have a soft dough. Place the dough on to a floured worktop, roll out evenly to about ½" (1cm) thick and cut out rounds. If you don't have a cutter, simply use a glass, but be sure to turn it in the flour before each cut to prevent the dough from sticking to the edges. I use an 3" (8cm) diameter cutter and get about six cakes.

Heat a frying pan or griddle with a large knob of lard. Get the fat hot enough for a speck of flour to hop and sizzle. Fry the cakes for 2–3 minutes each side. Serve hot or cold with a topping of your choice.

HIDDEN FRUIT CAKE

Many British wartime recipes used dried fruit or vegetables such as beets to sweeten cakes. Here's a 'hidden fruit cake' where I have used dates as a sweetener to reduce the sugar used but blended them to disguise the texture. Prunes work equally well.

ingredients

- 1 large egg
- 1 cup (100g) dates (rehydrate by adding ¾ cup (200ml) boiling water, leaving for an hour, then draining off the excess water and blending to a fine mush)
- 1 stick (110g) butter
- 2 cups all-purpose flour + 2 tsp baking powder (225g self-raising flour)
- ¼ cup (50g) sugar
- 5 tbsp milk

Method

Grease and line a 2lb (900g) loaf tin. Preheat the oven to 350°F/180°C/160°C fan/gas mark 4. Rub the butter into the flour and baking powder until it looks like breadcrumbs and then add the sugar, dates and egg. Incorporate the milk bit by bit and then spoon the cake mixture into the loaf tin and bake for about an hour or until a skewer inserted into the centre comes out clean. Turn out of the pan and cool on a wire rack. What you'll have is a honey-coloured, subtly sweet cake with an even spongy texture.

APPLE CAKE

Here's a cake sweetened this time entirely with apple, so the only sugar is a dash of apple fructose. It is very quick and easy to make. It works wonderfully with raisins and walnuts added.

ingredients

- 9oz (250g) stewed unsweetened eating apples/ apple sauce
- 1 stick (100g) softened butter
- 2 egg yolks
- 1¼ cups all-purpose flour + 1 heaped tsp baking powder (150g self-raising flour)
- 1 cup (100g) walnuts (optional)
- Pinch cinnamon (optional)
- ¾ cup (150g) raisins (optional)

Method

Grease and flour a 2lb (900g) loaf tin. Preheat the oven to 375°F/190°C/170°C fan/gas mark 5. If you are stewing the apples, use sweet eaters. Peel, core and slice, and sweat them down gently in a pan with a tight lid with as little added water as possible. Once cooled, blend the apples if they haven't already fallen to a mush. Then use a wooden spoon to blend the butter and the apple sauce thoroughly. Beat the egg yolks in a small bowl until light and fluffy, and fold into the apple sauce and butter, followed by the flour. Add the optional extras at this stage. Spoon the mixture into the tin and bake on the middle shelf for about 45 minutes or until a skewer or cocktail stick inserted into the centre of the cake comes out clean. Cool in the tin and then cut into slices.

VEGETABLE CRISPS

We have been making crisps (UK) or chips (US) out of vegetables for quite some time now, with varying degrees of success. The quality of bought crisps has improved over recent years but I do think that even the kettle-baked natural ones are over-salted and over-priced. These homemade crisps are quick and easy to make using lovely fresh vegetables and taste so wonderful you'll never go back to the packet kind again. Plus it's a great opportunity to explore veg with your child and figure out what it is about the texture that's altered on crisping. We tend to roast our crisps because pans of hot oil on a hob make me nervous. We have had success with parsnips, zucchini/courgette, carrots, sweet potatoes, eggplant/aubergine, beets, turnip, pumpkin, Jerusalem artichoke, celariac and the humble potato.

Henry won't eat kale crisps but will eat kale raw or steamed, and that goes for any type of cabbage. He'll eat zucchini steamed if the seeds are cut out but will eat the lot when they're crisps. Parsnips, eggplant and celeriac are preferred as crisps to any other way. So, on the whole, changing the texture by crisping has extended his vegetable repertoire. Here's how to make sweet potato chips.

ingredients

- 4 medium-sized sweet potatoes, peeled
- Olive oil
- Salt

Method

Preheat the oven to 350°F/180°C/160°C fan/gas mark 4. Using either the slicing side of a grater, a swivel peeler or a mandolin, cut the sweet potatoes into slices about 1/16" (1mm) thick. Then spread the slices out on paper towels, putting a double sheet over the top and pressing gently down to draw out the moisture. Basically, the drier they are, the crispier they cook. The slices can be left on the paper for an hour or two to thoroughly dry out, if that works with your day. Then place the slices in a large bowl and liberally cover with olive oil. Get your hands in there and make sure all the slices are covered. Lay out the slices in a single layer on a baking tray, sprinkle with salt and pop the tray into the oven, on the middle shelf. After 10 minutes, take out the tray and turn the crisps over. Then turn the oven up to 475°F/240°C/220°C fan/gas mark 9 and give them a quick blast for 2–5 minutes, depending on their thickness. This should crisp the sweet potato slices up nicely, but keep an eye on them because they will quickly burn. When your crisps look nice and golden, lay them out on a wire rack to cool.

If you want to serve a mixed tray of crisps, using a variety of vegetables, it is better to cook each vegetable type separately. If all cooked together the differing moisture content means uneven crisping and you'll get some cooked, some soggy and some burnt!

Don't stop at veggie crisps – try fruit crisps too! Apples, pears and bananas all work really well for us. I probably don't need to tell you to chop bananas and plantains with a knife to avoid making a mushy mess of your mandolin!

Protein-rich snacks

Of course, the anchor of a good snack is a chunk of protein, which, as I have already mentioned, has a massively positive effect on the mood and emotional wellbeing of my growing boy. Recently, I read a report by the nutritionist Casey Seidenberg[3] that took my breath away because it supported what I had seen happening with my child. The gist of it is that our brain needs four main chemicals – serotonin, endorphins, catecholamines and gamma-aminobutyric acid – to produce a steady flow of positive emotions. We get these chemicals from our food – and guess what? THEY ALL COME FROM PROTEIN. So protein = happy, as long as you don't mess it up by taking in too much of the stuff that sabotages it. Definitely, sugar = unhappy.

---

3   C. Seidenberg (2013) 'When they beg for a happy meal.' *Washington Post*. Available at www.washingtonpost.com/lifestyle/wellness/2013/02/26/eaf08e16-6f0e-11e2-8b8d-e0b59a1b8e2a_story.html, accessed on 18 September 2014.

Here are our top protein snacks: boiled eggs (great when you are out and about and come ready packed) and sliced meats (ham, turkey, beef or crispy bacon strips). Any nut butter is a fantastic snack: peanut, almond, Brazil, sunflower seed and macadamia butter. And that's only a sample – go into a good wholefood store and you'll see that there is a pretty impressive selection of nut butters. I graduated Henry from one butter to another by mixing a small amount of a new butter with a favourite one. Serve with carrot sticks or toast soldiers on the side.

PROTEIN BARS

Here's a protein bar that goes down very well and is super-healthy. It does contain brown rice syrup as a binding agent but, unlike conventional syrups, comes with the B vitamins thiamine, niacin and B6, and Vitamin K to name a few. The cocoa successfully masks the flavour of the coconut, dates and pecans.

ingredients

- 7oz (200g) dates
- Butter for greasing
- 1 cup (85g) oats
- ¼ cup (30g) unsweetened cocoa powder
- ¾ cup (65g) ground almonds
- 4oz (100g) pecans
- 5oz (150g) shredded coconut
- 1 tsp vanilla extract
- Pinch salt
- 6 tbsp brown rice syrup
- 1 stick (100g) butter

Method

In a small bowl, cover the dates with just-boiled water and set to one side. Grease an 8" (20cm) tin with a little butter. In a food processor, reduce the oats to fine pieces and then add the cocoa powder and ground almonds until all are mixed together thoroughly. Drain the dates and add those, together with the pecans, coconut, vanilla and salt. Next warm the syrup and butter gently in a large pan until it starts to bubble. Then add it to the other blended ingredients, either using the food processor or mixing thoroughly with a wooden spoon. Turn the thick dough into the buttered tin and pack it down firmly with the back of a metal spoon. Cool in the fridge for 2–3 hours before cutting into slices.

Do the shakey-shakey

I am very much a protein shake fan, but I prefer to use real foods in them, never protein powders, the like of which are used by bodybuilders to up their muscle bulk and vegetarians to complement their diet. This ready source of protein does seem like an easy fix to bolster the nutrient intake of a picky eater. But I'm not comfortable feeding protein formulated for adults to children and I would definitely recommend seeking advice from a doctor if you do intend to use them. The protein is extracted for these powders using extreme heat, which I understand can denature the delicate protein molecule and irreversibly change its form. Plus some have been found to harbour the chemicals used in the extraction process. Undoubtedly, not all powders are equal, some being less processed and safer than others. But why use a dehydrated, powdered protein with a shelf-life of a hundred years, potentially full of toxic nasties, when that same protein is readily available in real food? My favourite is whey cheese, commonly known as ricotta. It is a complete protein containing all the essential amino acids, which are the building blocks for feel-good brain chemicals and are used to build every new cell. Very few proteins have all of them, so whey cheese is pretty special stuff.

MILKSHAKES

ingredients
High-protein milkshake
- 1½ cups (300ml) whole milk
- 4oz (100g) ricotta cheese
- Cocoa powder to taste
- Agave to taste

Banana shake
- 1½ cups (300ml) whole milk
- 4oz (100g) ricotta cheese
- 2 ripe bananas
- Agave or honey to taste

Method
Combine all the ingredients with a hand blender. We don't use ice in our shakes as Henry prefers food at ambient temperature.

Try making up your own shakes. Start with the whole milk and ricotta and then add any other flavour that goes down well. Henry also likes a squirt of agave and a drop of natural vanilla extract. I know that a spoon of smooth peanut butter is loved by some children, just not mine. If your child eats berries, then brilliant – throw a handful in there. You can also switch out the cow's milk for goat's, oat, rice or almond milk. Henry is quite accustomed to the flavour of goat's milk, but other milks do need disguising with strong flavours.

Beware food additives

You can't always give your child the perfect homemade low-sugar, wholesome snack. I know that. But if you are out and about and need to get something, try to go for as natural and un-messed-with as possible, and steer clear of artificial colours, flavours and preservatives. Go for natural chips, oat biscuits, unsalted nuts or, best of all, a banana. You may have noticed that I always use butter instead of margarine. There's a great deal of discussion about which is better, but I would rather have straight dairy fat than a spread with flavours and emulsifiers.

Be wary of misleading labels: 'Contains no artificial flavours' does not mean the product doesn't contain other additives such as artificial colours, preservatives or flavour enhancers. The natural extension of this is to avoid coloured soap, toothpaste and bubble bath; according to the EU Scientific Committee on

Cosmetic Products,[4] colours can be absorbed through the skin, just as if you had eaten them. At best they are an inert foreign substance in our bodies; at worst carcinogenic.

Make the most of snack time

Snack time is a great opportunity to introduce new foods. There isn't the pressure that a mealtime brings with everyone sitting at the table, along with all the expectations and anxieties that come with eating in a social environment. A snack by definition is a small bite eaten in a casual setting, a great time to explore the next food on the 'to try' list. For a child who's not keen to try new foods, employ a bit of what I call 'attractive distraction'.

'Hey, let's see what your name looks like drawn in 3D and we're going to have rice cake for snack today.' (Not to be confused with my rice cake – this was the packet, biscuit variety.)

Henry would give me his characteristially cautious look as I set out paper, pencils and a rice cake on a plate.

'You like rice and this is just the same but all bunched together in a biscuit. How fantastic is that?'

I do sometimes make the mistake of being too cheery, and that has the effect of alerting Henry's suspicions. I wish I could be cooler about the process, but on days when I have five hundred things to do, my only alternative method is 'Just have a go and eat it, Henry,' said in world-weary tones, which never gets me anywhere.

Actually, I had no joy whatsoever with bought rice cakes. But that's just the texture likes and dislikes of my child. At eight, he would gladly shovel down a plate of chewy brown rice, but rice cakes with their dry brittleness were abhorrent to him and definitely to be given a wide berth. I tried making my own (see

---

4   Scientific Committee on Cosmetic Products and Non-Food Products Intended for Consumers (2002) 'Opinion of the Scientific Committee on Cosmetic Products and Non-Food Products Intended for Consumers Concerning the Safety Review of the Use of Certain Azo-Dyes in Cosmetic Products.' Available at http://ec.europa.eu/health/ph_risk/committees/sccp/documents/out155_en.pdf, accessed on 18 September 2014.

the recipe for rice fritters on page 58) and made them chewy to replicate cooked rice – he loves them. You may find the opposite is true for your child, but ideally they will get to like both because brown rice is a perfect carbohydrate for ASD kids: rich in manganese, which supports bone production and blood sugar control, as well as being a slow-release powerhouse, providing plenty of energy over a prolonged period of time.

I try to get Henry to eat a little bit of the snack whether he likes the idea of it or not, because sometimes he just decides, even before the food has connected with his taste buds, that this is going to be a bad experience. I see him make the grimace and go to spit it out before he's made a proper assessment of it. So inevitably deals are struck pre-snacking. That might be that he could have the snack he most favours if he also tries a teeny-tiny bit of this new food. I then big-up the new food in a way that appeals most.

It probably goes without saying that to encourage your child to eat a nutritious low-sugar diet, there has to be a whole family commitment to do the same. You are on to a loser if you are offering up a carrot stick as a mid-morning snack to your Asperger whilst an older sibling close by is stuffing in a giant Snickers bar. There can't be trashy off-limits food in your house, mainly because that just isn't fair. It's teaching your child double standards and it's also setting you up to fail in your objective to keep them physically and mentally healthy.

Drinks

Henry almost only drinks water and that's how we like it. Water is essential for every cell, organ and tissue in the body, and keeping the levels topped up can only be a good thing. A report by the British Psychological Society, detailing research by Chris Pawson and colleagues,[5] found that regularly hydrating the brain, which is itself 90 per cent water, actually makes you more intelligent.

---

5   British Psychological Society (2012) 'Can water boost your exam grades?' Available at www.bps.org.uk/news/can-water-boost-your-exam-grades, accessed on 18 September 2014.

Besides, the sugars in sodas, energy drinks and even kids' fruit juices make Henry hyperactive and so we've totally eliminated them from his diet. He does have diluted apple juice, but he's actually become so tuned in to how good water makes him feel and that has gone a long way to focusing his attentions on his need to rehydrate. Of course, Henry also downs pints of milk, and I will give him a protein shake when he's going through a growth spurt or he's not eaten well at mealtimes, but I categorize those as food.

Signs that your child isn't drinking enough water are headaches, lethargy and digestive issues. Overheated interiors, especially classrooms, a cultural shift towards kids drinking juice or sports drinks rather than plain water, compounded by a lack of body mindfulness in children, especially those with Asperger's, all contribute to dehydration. Henry has a problem recognizing when he is thirsty, so I have reiterated over and over that if his head hurts, drink a glass of water, and if he has yellow wee, drink a glass of water. I reckon at least five glasses of water a day is right for children. But that's a very rough estimate because water consumption depends on whether they are sedentary or active, the temperature and humidity of their environment and their age. So what I have encouraged with Henry is to take regular sips throughout the day and we have just made it a habit. It's hard to get an Aspie to do anything in moderation, but keeping the sips small and often maintains a healthily hydrated body without the need for frequent bathroom breaks which, in class, are bound to wind up the teacher. On school days Henry takes his 1 pint (600ml) water bottle with him and refills it when necessary. And after chatting with the teacher, she kindly allowed Henry to have his water bottle at his desk.

Chapter 6

Dinners that Work for Everyone

Part 1: Pick and Mix

Dinnertime used to be so stressful. I would frequently get up from the table and pace round the garden doing yoga breathing exercises having tried for an hour to gently persuade my weepy Asperger to eat something other than plain chicken: 'It's lovely, Henry. Just try a bit.' My husband, Dave, even resorted to lining up quarters along the table and offering to pay-per-bite, much to the indignation of his younger brother who invented food fads just to earn some cash. Henry was unmoved by bribes, threats or tales of starving Ethiopians and scabrous Victorian sailors with scurvy. But cooking with Henry worked, letting him bake the cake worked, and discovering the structure of a plant leaf got him eating kale.

Pick and mix dinners are perfect family meals shared with a child with Asperger's because everyone gets to tailor-make their own dish. Your child can start out with one or two of the meal's components making up their dinner and, as time goes on, progress by adding new elements. It even works well for the neurotypical members of my family. My husband and younger son, Will, share an obsessive love of chilli and would, if I let them, put chilli on everything they eat. So the chillis are in a separate bowl too! Of our favourite multi-dish dinners, Mexican is top of the list.

DiY FAJiTAS

A fajita is a soft wheat or corn tortilla wrapped around strips of meat, shredded salad leaves, vegetables, cheese, sour cream and pretty much anything else that takes your fancy, and they are absolutely delicious.

Here's what i usually include (some ingredients more typically Mexican than others!)

- Guacamole*
- Salsa*
- Refried beans*
- Creamed corn*
- Sour cream
- Grated cheese
- Lettuce, shredded
- Cilantro/coriander

- Jalapeño peppers
- Lime wedges
- Tortillas (corn or flour)*
- 2 large sirloin or rump steaks cut into strips*
- Chicken breast strips*
- ½ green cabbage, shredded and lightly steamed

*See recipes below.

This is a meal with dishes that span the full spectrum of the food experience from the basic and bland to colourful, spicy, multitextural and challenging, and everything in between. It is all part of my grand plan to expose Henry to those challenging and hated tastes and textures before easing him into eating them. I have had some success, but it has been a long haul. He started, aged seven, eating the plain tortilla with chicken on the side. Now, aged 11, he'll happily eat the beef, creamed corn, lettuce and cabbage. He's easing into guacamole and grated cheese but is yet to try refried beans and cilantro/coriander. I am working on the principle that since Aspergers have such rigid set behaviour patterns, familiarization is the only way forward. It just takes months and months.

I prepare the elements of our fajita dinner in the following order. I start with the guacamole, which I like to make fresh. Then the salsa and refried beans, followed by the creamed corn. Next I set out the small dishes of sour cream, grated cheese, shredded lettuce, cilantro, jalapeño peppers and lime wedges. Then the tortillas go into the oven to warm through while I fry the beef and chicken and steam the cabbage. Sounds like a heck of a juggle, I know, but some of these can be made beforehand. And never be shy about roping in willing helpers.

Classic guacamole

In my book it's nigh on sacrilege to eat a Mexican meal without guacamole. Henry will now have the smallest heap of guac on his plate and I see that as our greatest triumph, especially as it contains tomatoes, but we don't talk about that.

ingredients

- 2 ripe avocados
- 1 small red onion, finely chopped
- 2 garlic cloves, minced
- Large bunch cilantro/ coriander leaves, roughly chopped

- 1 tbsp lime juice (you can use lemon but lime tastes so much better)
- Large pinch salt
- 1 tomato, blanched in hot water to remove skin and then chopped very finely

Note: guacamole really should contain freshly chopped chillis but we serve ours on the side.

Method

I prefer not to include the stalks of the cilantro in guacamole. They do taste sweet, but their bluntness, I think, jars with the soft avocado.

Remove the skin and pit from the avocados and roughly mash them with a fork in a large, heavy mixing bowl, leaving some chunky bits. Add the chopped onion, garlic, coriander, lime and salt, and mash some more. Finally, add the chopped tomatoes.

A mix of red and green chillis are served in a bowl at my husband and younger son's end of the table.

I make my guacamole and serve it right away without chilling it. But if you need to store it for a while, hold off on adding the tomatoes. Cover the avocado mix with Saran Wrap/cling film to prevent the avocado oxidizing and going brown. Leave the tomatoes at room temperature where they will better keep their flavour and add them in just before serving.

Naturally, supply heaps of tortilla chips to accompany the guacamole. I buy organic blue tortilla chips that I first discovered in California many years ago. Quite apart from being absolutely delicious, they offer Henry that attractive bland carbohydrate with a twist. In the early days, the crunch of these tortilla chips introduced a new texture that paved the way for other crunchy food. One dinnertime, with our usual encouragement to try new fillings, he added tortilla chips to his tortilla wrap, which wasn't really what I had in mind, but at least it was a step in the right direction.

Pineapple salsa

It may be that Henry is 25 before he's spooning pineapple salsa on to his plate. But it is sitting there doing its job of being familiar, waiting for that day.

This is sweeter than your average salsa and the pineapple gives it a lovely tropical edge. The key here is to source really tasty tomatoes. Sometimes perfect-looking tomatoes are dull and bland, so go for flavour over looks every time. Don't be shy about getting your nose in there before you buy: the stronger and sweeter they smell, the better they taste.

ingredients

- 4 or 5 large ripe tomatoes, finely chopped
- 1lb (400g) pineapple, chopped (fresh is best but tinned will do)
- 1 small red onion, finely chopped
- Juice from half a fresh lemon
- Splash white wine vinegar
- Small bunch tarragon leaves, finely chopped
- Large bunch cilantro/coriander, leaves and stalks finely chopped
- Salt and pepper to taste

Method

In a medium bowl, combine all ingredients and then cover for at least an hour to blend the flavours. Drain before serving.

Refried beans

This is the perfect food to make in bulk on a rainy Sunday and freeze in meal-sized portions for another day. Mine is a bland version of what ought to be a fragrant, spicy dish to give it the maximum chance of being eaten by my boy.

I use bacon fat to fry the beans and it gives them the most fantastic flavour. So the next time you fry bacon, tip the fat off into a small pot or bowl and keep it for up to a week in the fridge.

ingredients

- 2 tbsp bacon fat or lard
- 1 onion, finely chopped
- 2 tsp ground cumin
- ½ tsp paprika
- 1 tbsp tomato puree
- 1 tsp dark brown sugar1 tbsp balsamic vinegar
- 15oz (400g) can black beans, drained and rinsed
- 15oz (400g) can pinto or kidney beans, drained and rinsed
- Pinch salt and pepper
- ¾ cup (200ml) water

Method

Heat 1 tbsp of the bacon fat or lard in a heavy-based frying pan and soften the onion for about 5 minutes before stirring in the spices, tomato puree, sugar and vinegar. Tip in the beans with the salt and pepper and the water. Bubble gently for about 20 minutes until the water has almost evaporated. Take the beans out of the pan and mash two-thirds of the beans with a fork or potato masher until they become a smooth thick paste. Add the rest of the fat to the pan and return the mushed beans and the whole beans and fry on a high heat for 5 more minutes.

Mrs Barr's creamed corn

Creamed corn isn't a Mexican dish but corn does feature in many forms in Mexican cooking. That's my excuse and I'm sticking to it. Fact of the matter is, Henry intensely dislikes the texture of sweetcorn nibbles but isn't averse to creamed corn. He was converted, aged nine, after a particularly sumptuous Thanksgiving luncheon courtesy of our friends, the Barrs. He'll now eat a dollop of it on a side plate. Mrs Barr kindly emailed the recipe a couple of days ago.

Preparation time: 30 minutes
Yield: 4 servings

ingredients

- 8 ears of fresh corn, shucked
- ½ cup (120ml) cream or half and half (a mixture of milk and cream)
- 2 tbsp butter
- Salt and pepper to taste

Method

1. Cut or grate the kernels off of the corncob into a mixing bowl. (Grating works better, but is messier.)

2. Add the cream or half and half to the corn kernels.

3. Melt the butter in a heavy skillet. Add the corn and cream mixture. Cook on medium high heat, scraping the skillet on a regular basis. The corn should stick slightly before being scraped, helping to thicken the starches and cream.

4. When golden, add salt and pepper to taste.

Mrs Barr also swears blind that at that fabulous Thanksgiving dinner Henry also partook of her rather tasty creamed spinach. So, as an added bonus, here it is:

Mrs Barr's creamed spinach

Preparation time: 30 minutes
Yield: 4 servings

ingredients

- 2 cups (350g) boiled or panned spinach (see steps 1 and 2 below)
- 1½–2 tbsp butter
- 1 clove garlic
- 2 tbsp olive oil
- 1 tbsp finely chopped onion
- 1 tbsp all-purpose flour
- ½ cup (100ml) hot cream or stock
- ½ tsp sugar
- Salt and pepper to taste
- ¼ tsp dry mustard

Method

1. Use the boiled method if spinach is old and tough: Cut the tough roots and stems from 1lb (500g) of spinach. Wash it until it is free from sand and soil. Place spinach in 2 cups (500ml) of rapidly boiling water. Reduce heat and simmer, covered, for about 10 minutes until tender.

2. Use the panned method if spinach is young and tender: Remove the coarse stems from 1lb (500g) of spinach. Shake off as much water as possible. In a large heavy skillet, heat 1 tablespoon butter and 2 tablespoons olive oil. Add the spinach. Cover the skillet and cook over a high heat until steam appears. Reduce heat and simmer until tender, 5–6 minutes in all.

3. Blend, rice or chop the prepared spinach to a fine puree.

4. Rub a skillet with a clove of garlic and melt the remaining butter in the skillet. Add the onion to the melted butter and cook until golden.

5. Stir in the flour until blended. Slowly stir in the cream or stock and the sugar.

6. When the sauce is smooth and hot, add the spinach. Stir and cook for 3 minutes. Add the salt, pepper and mustard.

Tortillas

I go for a corn tortilla simply because it's an opportunity to have a wheat-free meal. According to the packets, corn tortillas do have more magnesium than the wheat, although not as much iron and calcium. Corn tortillas, as you might expect, have more fibre, essential for a healthy gut.

I did have a go at making tortillas with fine polenta and they are simple enough to make, but then I discovered that the best-quality shop-bought ones are just as good and a heck of a lot easier. To warm them, pile up about five or six and with your fingers sprinkle the tiniest amount of water between each layer. Wrap them all up in aluminium foil and place in a pre-heated oven at 350°F/180°C/160°C fan/gas mark 4 for about 15 minutes. I usually put in another batch just as we are eating so warm ones are ready mid-meal.

Beef and chicken

Properly, I should marinate the beef or chicken to give it a spicy, tangy edge, but that won't work for us. So the meat simply gets cut into slivers 2–3" (5–8cm) long and fried at very high temperature for barely 2 minutes for the beef and 10 or so minutes for chicken.

Lay it all out

This meal looks so pretty with the red and yellow salsa, yellow creamed corn, browns of the meat, green chillis and cabbage, and the blue tortillas! Add bowls of Mexican fixings, such as sour cream, grated cheese, fresh roughly chopped cilantro/coriander, chilli peppers, lime wedges and basically anything else you fancy. I get Henry to smell the contents of the bowls and we talk about where each food comes from, how it is grown and anything else to draw him in and get him to regard these foods as safe and familiar. This is life-affirming food; I love it and it warms my heart to see Henry begin to love it too.

SELF-ASSEMBLY PAD THAI

My assessment of a Thai or pan-Asian restaurant is based on the quality of their Pad Thai. It's a dish I know well and love, but at home I do simplify the preparation to save time and adapt it for our own needs. I have an impressive selection of small bowls collected over the years. None match, most have chips and each has a story. They all get to appear en masse for this dish, holding its separate elements ready to be assembled in whatever way you wish. And at the risk of repeating myself ad nauseam, it gives Henry the opportunity to mix textures by slow degrees while exposing him to other foods and flavours.

ingredients
Pad Thai sauce

- 1 tbsp tamarind paste, dissolved in ½ tbsp warm water
- 1 tbsp fish sauce
- 3 tbsp sweet chilli sauce
- 2 tbsp palm sugar
- Pinch pepper

Noodles, chicken and vegetables

- 10oz (400g) Thai brown rice noodles
- Vegetable oil for stir-frying
- 14oz (400g) chicken (or beef/tofu/duck), cut into 1" (2cm) lengths
- 1 cup (200ml) chicken stock
- 4 cloves garlic, finely chopped
- 2 fresh red or green chillies, finely chopped
- 7oz (200g) fresh bean sprouts
- 3 scallions/spring onions, sliced
- Small bunch fresh cilantro/ coriander
- Small bowl of crushed or roughly chopped peanuts (or other nuts, such as cashews)
- Wedges of lime

Method

Start out by making the sauce. This is what gives the Pad Thai its unique flavour; it is very strong and pungent and really for the benefit of those who wish to spice up their own meal. In a small pan, combine all the sauce ingredients and heat gently until the sugar has dissolved. The key to success in cooking Thai dishes, I have been told by my lovely Thai friend Ratikka, is to balance the sweetness, sourness, spiciness and saltiness. So taste the sauce, noting, for instance, whether the sour tamarind is overpowering the other flavours. Adjust the elements accordingly, but do be careful to add only the smallest amounts in your efforts to rebalance the flavours – otherwise, you could end up with a bucket load of sauce!

Cook the rice noodles according to the instructions on the packet and take care not to overcook them. Most instructions will give you a boiling time for noodles that are to be fried and this is the timing you need. Drain and rinse with cold water and set aside for later.

Set your oven at 325°F/160°C/140°C fan/gas mark 3 and put in two medium-sized ovenproof dishes that will be used later to keep the noodles and chicken warm while you fry the other ingredients. Next, heat a heavy-based frying pan or wok over a medium heat with a liberal splash of oil. In this case, my staple olive most definitely won't work. Sesame or peanut oils are great here, but sunflower or canola/rapeseed are also fine. Add the chicken and cook for a couple of minutes, then add about half of the chicken stock and keep frying for a further 5 minutes until the chicken is cooked through. Remove the chicken from the frying pan and put it into the warmed dish and then back in the oven, covered with foil so it doesn't dry out.

Add a little more oil to the pan and then fry the noodles for only about a minute, tossing them about the pan with two spatulas or two forks, as you would toss a salad, to make sure they cook evenly. Add the rest of the chicken stock and cook on high for another minute turning the noodles frequently again. Take the noodles and place in the other warmed dish, covering with foil and return to the oven.

Quickly toss the garlic and chilli around the pan and spoon into a small bowl; also heat the sauce through and place in a bowl. Note that I fry the spicier elements last so they don't flavour the blander ingredients such as the noodles.

The constituents of the Pad Thai are now all ready, and on your table you should have: a large bowl of chicken and a large bowl of noodles, and then lots of small bowls with garlic and chilli, raw bean sprouts and scallions/spring onions, fresh cilantro/coriander, chopped nuts, lime wedges and the Pad Thai sauce. It looks lovely all laid out, and little bits tried here and there or even just smelled will go a long way to retraining those ASD taste buds!

Note: My top tip is to grow your own bean sprouts. So easy, so cheap, so nutritious. Soak a large handful of dried mung beans overnight and drain. Use a glass bowl to let the light in and cover with Saran Wrap/cling film, making a few holes in the top. That will kept them from drying out but still allow the air to circulate. Rinse and drain once a day and keep them on a window ledge or somewhere sunny. In a day or two, you'll have masses of sprouting beans that are so good in salads or stir-fries. Then, mark my words, you'll become a sprouting nutter and try all sorts of seeds: broccoli, lentils, chickpeas... If your child helps you grow them, I can guarantee they will be far more open to trying them.

LAMB SATAY

I can't remember when we discovered that food, to my boy, was just that bit more interesting when served on a stick. Almost any meat will be eaten if it is on a stick. I started out by serving just plain grilled lamb on bamboo skewers, then tried beef, duck and a whole host of vegetables. In my mission to educate Henry's taste buds, I introduced a soy and teriyaki marinade so weak that you or I would hardly detect it. The great thing with a marinade is that it's a flavour that you can't see, if that makes any sense at all. Gradually, as Henry's palate grew accustomed to the flavours, I made the marinade a little bit stronger. He'll now eat meat when it has been marinated in soy, teriyaki sauce, ginger and garlic, and although it is still mild compared to how the rest of us would like, it is fun to have this dish as a dinner we can all enjoy. I think the stick must act as a distraction, because it has allowed me to add flavours to the meat that otherwise would be rejected. Pick and choose which ones your child will eat; if the answer is 'none', then just make the plain lamb and gradually introduce these flavours at a later date.

ingredients

- 1lb (450g) lamb, diced into 1" (2cm) cubes
- Bamboo skewers (I use small ones about 8" (20cm) long)

Marinade

- 1 tbsp soy sauce
- 1 tbsp teriyaki sauce
- 1 clove garlic, minced
- ½" (1cm) ginger root, finely chopped
- Olive oil for cooking

My easy peanut sauce

- 2 tbsp smooth peanut butter
- 2 tbsp warm water
- 2 tbsp rice vinegar
- 1 tbsp dark soy sauce
- 1 tbsp Thai sweet chilli sauce
- ½ tbsp palm sugar

Method

I always make sure that the lamb chunks are fat-free and gristle-free because a gristly piece of meat can upset the whole experience. First, thread the lamb on to the bamboo skewers, using about two-thirds of their length. This much lamb should fill about 10 skewers. Then lay the skewers in a single layer in a shallow dish that neatly contains all of the skewers. Next, prepare the marinade, which has the effect of tenderizing and flavouring the lamb, although only slightly in our case. Mix all the ingredients of the marinade together and use a pastry brush to coat all sides of the lamb. Cover the dish with Saran Wrap/cling film and leave in the fridge for at least an hour. The longer you leave it, the more the flavours will be absorbed by the meat.

For the peanut dipping sauce, dissolve the sugar in the warm water and then whisk all the ingredients together. If you like a thinner sauce, add a little more warm water. Serve in a shallow dish so the lamb satay skewers can be easily covered. Henry will try a bit of this on the side of his plate.

To cook the lamb, take the skewers out of the marinade and rinse the meat, washing off the marinade. Then thoroughly dry the lamb with paper towels. As you progress with stronger flavours, try leaving the marinade on the meat. Washing just removes the marinade taste that may have concentrated on the outside of the lamb. Make sure the skewers get wet too as this prevents them from burning under the grill. Crank your grill up to high and cook for 5 minutes on each side. Serve as an accompaniment to Pad Thai or with some lovely brown rice and crisp veggies.

PIZZA-U-LIKE

This is such a feel-good dinner and a perfect one if the boys have friends over.

The pizzas are made at the table and, because the bases are fresh out of the oven, finely grated cheese melts nicely to make the pizzas look sufficiently authentic. Again, this is a great way to empower your child and give them control over what they eat and how they mix it up.

You can find really excellent pizza dough mixes and, let's face it, you can also buy the bases already made (I am not judging you). Either of these options is perfectly fine. If you want to make the bases from scratch, though, here's how. I do make a conventional base because while you can monkey around with breads for school lunches and protein cakes, pizza doesn't taste quite like pizza unless the base is traditional.

Henry has accepted the tomato base because it is smooth, without bits. For the toppings, he'll go for a little cheese and ham every time. But that's progress: once upon a time the bread base was all that would be eaten.

For the dough

ingredients

- 4 cups (500g) white bread flour (use '00' fine grade as it makes a smoother dough)
- ⅔ cup (100g) semolina flour
- Pinch salt

- ¼oz (7g/1 sachet) dried yeast
- 2 tbsp (25ml) olive oil
- ¼ cup (50ml) warm milk
- 1⅓ cups (350ml) warm water

Method

Mix the dry ingredients together in a large bowl, then use a fork to gradually stir in the olive oil, milk and water. Dust your hands and worktop with flour and turn the dough out and start kneading.

Use a pull, roll and fold action, turning the dough a fraction as you go to knead in all sides evenly. Do this for a good 10 minutes to stretch the gluten. When the dough feels light and springy, place it in a large clean bowl with Saran Wrap/cling film or a damp tea towel over the top and leave in a warm place until it has doubled in size – about an hour. Peel the dough out of the bowl on to a clean, floured surface and knead again to knock all the air out until you have a nice smooth, spongy dough again. Then divide into eight balls. I make eight small pizzas but you can make four normal-sized ones or two huge ones. Roll each ball out, thinner if you like them crispy, thicker if you are going for that deep-pan effect. Then place the pizza bases on oiled metal trays. I always add the first coat of tomato sauce, which is easy enough to make and tastes five million times better than even the best jar sauce (see recipe below). Then the bases, with a smearing of tomato sauce, go into a hot oven at about 475°F/240°C/220°C fan/gas mark 9 for no more than 7 or 8 minutes. Pizzas for the children should instantly go on a cold plate so they don't burn themselves on the metal cooking tray.

For the tomato sauce

ingredients

- 4 tbsp olive oil
- 2 cloves garlic, finely chopped
- 2 red onions, finely chopped
- 2 carrots, finely chopped
- 2 young celery stalks, finely chopped
- Bunch fresh parsley, roughly chopped
- Small bunch fresh basil, chopped
- Pinch salt and pepper
- 5lb (2kg) fresh ripe tomatoes (the most flavoursome you can get), finely chopped

Method

Heat the oil in a saucepan and fry all the ingredients apart from the tomatoes for 20 minutes until soft and partly caramelized. Add the tomatoes and cook for a further 20 minutes, stirring to prevent the mixture sticking to the pan. Add a little water if the sauce does start to get tacky on the bottom. When it is nicely reduced and aromatic, take it off the heat. You can blend the tomato and vegetable mixture to achieve an evenly chopped sauce, but since I am after an even smoother texture, I put it through a fine sieve to strain out all the bits and I am left with a wonderful, fragrant tomato sauce, perfect on a pizza or with pasta. Return to the pan and continue to cook the strained sauce for a thicker consistency.

Topping options

- Grated cheese
- Fresh basil
- Raw or cooked spinach
- Ham
- Chopped fried chicken
- Pulled pork
- Salami
- Red onion
- Anchovy
- Olives and capers

PLOUGHMAN'S DINNER

This is really a bit of a no-brainer of a meal when attempting to feed a mix of super-sensitive and regular palates. Just lay out the table as you would a buffet and everyone makes up their own plate. Any ploughman's is always improved with a homemade bread and a pork pie (recipe below). Now Henry will eat six things on the ploughman's list and the aim, of course, is to add to his selection.

Components

- Bread (the soya and quinoa recipes are on pages 45–48)
- Apple slices
- Roast beef
- Pork pie (see recipe below)
- Watercress
- Carrot sticks
- Radish
- Onion
- Tomato
- Large chunks of Cheddar, Brie, Stilton, etc.
- Scallions/spring onions
- Beets
- Chutneys
- Celery sticks
- Pickled onions

PORK PIE MRS PATTEN

Being able to eat a pork pie as a pork pie is fairly recent. Up until about a year ago, I would present the pie to Henry as pork and crust – two separate items on his plate. I don't make my pies with jelly, but if we're having a bought pie, that jelly is removed, as this texture is definitely a 'no' for him. Gradually, Henry progressed from eating the separated crust and meat to eating the crust from around the pie because a crust comes away from pork meat very easily. Several pork pies later, small bits of meat were being consumed as part of large mouthfuls of pastry. By very slow degrees over a number of pork pie dinners, more meat was part of the pastry bites until one day Henry just ploughed through the whole slice, eating meat and pastry together. This process of desensitization allowed the combination of the pork and crust textures to become less and less of an issue until finally, almost two years after starting out with separate pork and pastry, Henry was able to take a bite of whole pie. Success!

ingredients

Filling

- 2½lb (1kg) pork (ask your butcher for half shoulder, half belly, as the fat in the belly adds superb flavour)
- Pinch salt
- Butter for greasing

Pastry

- 4 cups (500g) all-purpose flour
- Pinch salt
- 3oz (80g) lard
- ½ stick (60g) butter
- 1oz (20g) beef suet (if you have trouble getting hold of suet substitute lard here)
- ¾ cup (220ml) hot water
- 1 egg, for glazing

Method

This pie is best made in an 8" (20cm) round cake tin where the sides can be removed from the base. A regular tin will work just as well but there is a bit more jiggling involved to get it out. Lightly butter the tin.

Then prepare the meat. I like having some chunky bits and the rest a sausage consistency. So chop a third of the shoulder roughly into ½–1" (1–2cm) cubes and then use a meat grinder or food processor to grind the rest. Mix the chunks and ground pork together with the salt and transfer to the fridge.

Next make the pastry. Take a large heavy mixing bowl and combine the flour and salt. In a pan over a moderate heat, add the lard, butter and suet to the hot water and bring to the boil, stirring continuously. Gradually mix the boiled water and fat into the flour with a fork. As it cools, it should form a lovely smooth dough. If it is too floppy to work with, give it 10 minutes to cool in the fridge.

Flour your work surface. Cut away a quarter of the pastry and set it to one side. Roll out the big bit of pasty into a giant circle. It helps to have the cake tin in front of you so that you can visualize the area in the centre of the pastry that will form the base and the width required to take the pastry up the sides of the tin. I always make the pastry circle just a little too big and then gently fold it in half so it is easier to lift. Place the pastry in the tin and press the centre around the base; mould the rest up the sides, with some flopping over the top. Don't fret about any tears, just cut away some of the extra over the sides and push it into place. There shouldn't be any holes or the meat will bulge out of the pastry. Fill the middle with the meat. Roll the lid and place it on the top, pinching the side and lid pastry together with your thumb and fingers and then cut away the excess. Make a hole for the steam to escape right in the middle of the lid with the end of a wooden spoon and use any off-cuts to decorate the top. Finally, brush the lid with a little beaten egg. Cook for 30 minutes at 350°F/180°C/160°C fan/gas mark 4 and then reduce the heat to 325°F/160°C/140°C fan/gas mark 3 for a further 90 minutes. Leave to cool before removing from the tin.

Actually, this pork pie straddles this and the next chapter rather nicely: whilst working as an element of the ploughman's, it also fits the remit for the following chapter of cooking dishes that can be served as separate elements but on the same plate.

Chapter 7

Dinners that Work for Everyone

Part 2: Favourite Separate Texture Meals

With the pick-and-mix meals, I try to encourage Henry to actively combine foods by selecting them from the serving dishes on the table and creating mixes that end up as a single mouthful. Drawing these elements together, he gets to experience various texture combinations, which are becoming more complex over time. This chapter takes that concept a step further by presenting separate textures on the same plate, something that used to be utterly challenging for him. By putting the different components on the same plate, albeit apart, I am forcing the close proximity of foods that he wouldn't necessarily place together. The foods don't need to be eaten together, but the fact that they sit side by side is a big thing. I usually have four components to the meal: three of them Henry is completely comfortable with and one is new or actively disliked.

MILD CHICKEN CURRY

Chicken curry was our first big success adding sauce. For the longest time I served the chicken and curry sauce separately. Henry ate the chicken with a small dab of sauce on the side. It took three years to go from no sauce to loads of sauce – that is, a proper chicken curry.

ingredients

- Vegetable oil for frying
- 8 chicken thighs on the bone
- 1 clove garlic, finely chopped
- 1 tsp ground cumin
- 1 tsp ground cilantro/ coriander
- 1 tsp ground cardamom

- ½" (1cm) chunk of fresh root ginger, peeled and grated
- ½ tsp ground turmeric
- 1 tsp mild chilli powder
- Pinch salt
- ½ cup (100ml) chicken stock
- 1 tbsp almond flour
- 1½ cups (400ml) coconut milk

method

In a large frying pan on a high heat, add a hefty slug of oil and then fry the chicken legs in their skin. Sear all sides and then turn the heat down to medium and cook thoroughly, which should take around 45 minutes. Check that the legs are cooked through by poking a metal skewer into the fleshiest part and press to see if the juices run clear. It's difficult to overcook and dry out fried chicken as the oil seals in the moisture; anyway, it is better to overcook than undercook chicken.

While the chicken is frying, make the sauce. In another frying pan, heat a tablespoon of oil over a low heat and gently soften the garlic for 5 minutes before adding the cumin, cilantro/coriander, cardamom, ginger, turmeric, chilli powder and salt. Stir these around in the pan and then add half of the chicken stock and keep stirring. At this stage I usually give the sauce a blast with the hand blender to smooth out the consistency and then return it to the pan. Next add the almond flour and the coconut milk and the rest of the stock. Cook for a further 10–20 minutes to reduce the sauce and then set to one side off the heat. The chicken should be ready now.

To make life easier, of course, you can use chicken breast or leg meat cut off the bone which just needs cutting up and frying. But if you fry the meat on the bone first, the chicken has so much more flavour and is really succulent. It easily comes away from the bone and might need one last blast in the frying pan to warm it through. Present your child's chicken initially without the sauce and then gradually, with each subsequent curry, coat it with ever-increasing amounts of the sauce until they will happily take the chicken curry as it was intended to be eaten! We serve it with brown rice and broccoli.

TOAD BY THE HOLE

Henry embraced proper sausages after a thorough investigation into sausage casings. As I mentioned in an earlier chapter, frankfurters worked because they have no discernible skin and the texture is consistent from the outside in. Since casings were the barrier (ha!) to Henry enjoying a regular sausage, we became veritable sausage skin experts in our quest to find the least rubbery sausage skin. There are two camps for casings: natural and artificial. Most bangers nowadays have a man-made casing, which can be collagen to mimic the natural kind, cellulose from cotton or wood pulp (euw) or plastic. You are obviously supposed to peel the plastic casings off before consuming the meat and these are usually used for bigger sausages such as salamis. The cellulose and collagen casings can be rather elastic and chewy. Natural sausage skins, made from the intestines of sheep, pigs and cattle, are semi-permeable and absorb the juices and flavour of the meat. This means they soften on cooking, which goes a long way to making them less discernible from the texture of the sausage.

For regular-sized sausages, pig's intestines are used because the casing has to be strong to prevent splitting during cooking. Even though they are an improvement on the artificial skins, these sausages have a tough sheath to get through before you reach the sausage meat. But we found that chipolatas cased in sheep intestines were by far the best as sheep gut is thinner and finer than the alternatives and forms an almost imperceptible covering to the sausage. Henry will eat these without any fuss at all. Check the ingredients list. Some manufacturers will state the nature of the casing; otherwise, search the internet for the brand if you want to check before you buy.

I have considered making my own sausages but I have not quite got there yet. It seems to me that buying a sausage maker is quite a commitment to sausages. We'll see. So for now I buy the best chipolatas I can find: always free-range, usually organic. Ones that are made with good-quality meat are less likely to contain chewy or gristly bits, the discovery of which are a disaster at the dinner table. You'll be paying more for your sausages but they will get eaten, especially if you make a 'hole' to go with them!

ingredients

Toad

- Butter or olive oil for frying
- 2 or 3 sausages per person (and I usually cook at least 6 extra to eat cold the next day)
- 2 large onions, peeled and cut into slices

Hole

- 1 cup (100g) all-purpose flour
- Pinch salt
- 2 large eggs, beaten
- 1 cup (250ml) reduced-fat milk (or ¾ cup (200ml) whole milk and ¼ cup (50ml) cold water)
- 1 tbsp oil

Method

Put a thick-based pan on a medium heat with a knob of butter or a little oil. Prick the sausage skins on all sides with a cocktail stick to stop them splitting and fry gently for 20–30 minutes depending on their size, turning to cook each side. I know that sausages don't have sides but you know what I mean! Chipolatas sometimes cook in 10 minutes. Always test one by cutting it in half to check it's cooked through. Whilst the sausages are cooking, prepare the batter for the hole. Set the oven at 425°F/220°C/200°C fan/ gas mark 7.

In a large bowl, mix the flour and salt and then use a fork or whisk to gradually add the eggs and then the milk (or milk and water) until you have a lovely smooth batter. Next, take a large ovenproof dish (I use a metal roasting pan), pour in about a tablespoon of oil and tip the pan so it coats up the sides where the batter will rise. Put the roasting pan in the oven for 5 minutes to heat the oil. This gives a crispier outer edge to the cooked batter. Take out the pan, now very hot, pour in the batter and return to the oven. Cook for 20 minutes – more if you like it brown and crispy, less if you like it soggy in the middle! Cut into slices and serve it straight from the roasting pan. I have been known to prepare a second batter ready to pour into the empty dish that's ready just as everyone has finished their first helping and are asking for seconds!

Five minutes from the sausages being ready, I add the onions to the pan and they cook beautifully in the juices from the sausages. Kale or cabbage are perfect accompanying vegetables. Henry eats all of the above separately, apart from the onions, which sit shunned on the side of the plate.

Having approved chipolatas, Henry has worked up to tougher casings and new flavours and will now eat sausages made with wild boar, chicken, turkey, duck, buffalo and venison, along with the standard pork ones. Apple in a sausage is accepted, as are some herbed ones where the texture of the herbs is indistinguishable from that of the meat. But sausages with, say, rosemary in them won't fly as the rosemary has a hard woodiness in contrast to the soft sausage meat – a texture too far. Experiment with your sausages and find out what works for you. If you have a friendly butcher, he might sell you a variety pack!

HAM, BROAD BEANS AND BOILED POTATOES

Henry hates broad beans and will do just about anything to get out of eating them. The rubbery skin enclosing a soft, pulpy interior is a total turn-off. But now he's aged 11, I am becoming a little more militant with the broad-ening of his vegetable repertoire. Basically, I am serving a hated vegetable with another favourite food – in this case, free-range ham steak fried to perfection with all the fat and crispy bits cut off, leaving succulent, even-textured, sweet, salty meat. And here's where I tough-love him, because to eat the steak he has to eat the beans – not a huge hill of beans, just a small pile. We've had the discussion about how this works and we've had the weeping and wailing, but now he just accepts the deal. There are limits, though, and it is important not to push too far. For instance, I could serve cherry tomatoes with chocolate cake or fluffy white bread and he wouldn't touch them.

FISH PIE

This is a great meal for ASD children because the fish and piecrust are cooked together but easily separated. There is an extra cooking stage for the part of the pie for the rest of the family that adds a creamy sauce, a texture that is still on our 'to do' list.

ingredients
For the fish centre

- 1lb (500g) mild-tasting fish such as coley, tilapia or halibut, filleted and bone-checked, cut into 2" (5cm) lengths
- ⅔ cup (150ml) fish stock (see below)

- ½ stick (50g) butter
- Pinch salt
- ⅔ cup (150ml) heavy cream
- 1 tbsp chopped parsley

Pastry

- ⅔ cup (300g) all-purpose flour
- Pinch salt

- 1 stick (100g) butter
- 2oz (50g) lard
- 6 tbsp cold water

Method

First make the fish stock. Put any bones, off-cuts, tail-ends or skin in a pan with 1½ cups (350ml) water and simmer gently for 30 minutes. Then make the pastry. Mix the flour and salt in a bowl. Chop the butter and lard into small cubes and rub into the flour until it resembles breadcrumbs. Using a knife, mix the water into the flour until it forms a smooth pastry dough. Cover the bowl with Saran Wrap/cling film to prevent it from drying out and put it in the fridge.

Set the oven at 425°F/220°C/200°C fan/gas mark 7. Use an ovenproof, shallow pie dish (mine is 8" (20cm) square). Grease it with butter and then place the fish pieces all along the bottom and cover with the strained fish stock. Take the pastry dough out of the fridge and roll out on a floured board until it is big enough to generously fit over the top of the dish. Place the pastry over the dish and use a fork to press down along the edges to seal it on to the dish. Using a knife, slice the excess pastry off, leaving ½" (1cm) or so overlap to allow for shrinkage. Make a hole in the top of the pastry to let out the steam and pop it in the oven for 20 minutes.

Meanwhile, heat the cream until almost boiling and mix with the parsley. When the pastry turns a lovely golden brown, remove the pie from the oven. Cut through a quarter of the pastry and remove this to your child's plate, then scoop out the same proportion of fish and place it on the plate a decent distance from the pastry. Now take the remainder of the pie, lift the piecrust and pour the cream and parsley mixture over the fish. Replace the crust and return the pie to the oven for 5 more minutes. Serve with carrots.

LATKAS WITH SALMON

These are splendid fried potato pancakes traditionally cooked by Jews on Hanukkah. We lived in a Jewish, Christian and Muslim neighbourhood in the Midwest, and I used to make these at Christmas time just to mix it up a little bit and celebrate where we were.

ingredients

- 4 or 5 medium potatoes, peeled
- 1 small onion, finely chopped
- 2 egg yolks
- Pinch salt
- 1 tbsp matzo meal or crackers smashed to small bits
- 2 tbsp all-purpose flour
- Corn or sunflower oil for frying

Method

First grate the potatoes. I prefer a finer grater but a coarser shredded potato also works well. Grate the potato into water, which prevents browning and also flushes out most of the potato starch. Take the grated potatoes out of the water and let them drain through a colander for a few minutes. Then tip the potato out on to a clean tea towel and wring out the rest of the water. You might need another tea towel to take out all the moisture. I love onion in our latkas, but in order for it to fly under Henry's radar, the onion has to be chopped really fine. Add the onion in with the potatoes and then mix in the egg yolks, a pinch of salt and the matzo or regular cracker meal. On a floured wooden board or tray set about shaping the individual pancakes. I use a tablespoon-sized heap, make a ball, place it in the flour and flatten it with the back of a flour-coated spoon. When you have your batch of potato latkas all lined up, heat up a large frying pan with ½" (1cm) of oil in the bottom. It is better to use an oil with a high smoke point – that is, one that can be heated to a high temperature without browning, such as corn, sunflower, grape-seed or canola/rapeseed oil. Place a small grated piece of potato into the oil; if it dances and fizzles, you are ready to cook. With a wide metal spatula, transfer the potato pancakes into the oil and cook for a maximum of 2–3 minutes each side until nicely browned. Once cooked, transfer to a warm plate.

Latkas are wonderful served with smoked salmon, red onion rings, al dente green beans, fish roe and a large blob of sour cream. Henry started out by eating the latkas just by themselves as he seemed to accept them as a kind of bread, especially if I upped the matzo meal. Gradually, we encouraged him to add something else. For three years it was just the latkas with a few green beans and then he worked up to salmon, which was flash-fried smoked salmon because he can't take the texture of the raw stuff. The sour cream is a very late addition and he'll only eat the smallest dab placed right on the outer rim of his plate.

Favourite dinner desserts

APPLE PIE

I make apple pie in a way that enables it to be deconstructed for Henry. Once cooked, the pastry lid of the pie comes off quite easily so in his bowl he has the apples to one side and the crust to the other. I use eating apples so there's no need to add sugar to the apples, but I do sweeten the pastry ever so slightly.

ingredients

- 2 cups (230g) all-purpose flour (¾ spelt/¼ all-purpose works well)
- Pinch salt
- 1 stick (50g) butter, cubed
- 2oz (50g) lard cubed
- 2 tsp maple syrup
- 7 or 8 eating apples, peeled, quartered, cored and sliced
- 1 egg, beaten

Method

Preheat the oven to 400°F/200°C/180°C fan/gas mark 6.

Start off by making the pastry. In a large bowl (I like to use a heavy ceramic one that doesn't scoot about the work surface), mix the flour and salt, then gently rub in the butter and lard with your fingers. Dissolve the maple syrup in 2 tablespoons of cold water, add to the bowl and use a knife to mix everything together until you have a nice smooth dough. Cover the bowl in Saran Wrap/cling film and place it in the fridge for 30 minutes.

I like the apples in chunky slices – say ½" (1cm) thick – so they cook apace with the pastry. I use a shallow square dish that's 2" (5cm) deep and about 8" (20cm) across. Because I don't line the dish with pastry, you might argue that this isn't technically a pie and you may have a point. All I know is that I can push this 'pie' out in 20 minutes and there's no messing about fitting the base, trimming and bonding the base to the lid. It is also especially easy to deconstruct. Lay the apples evenly in the dish and sprinkle over a tablespoon of water. Retrieve the pastry from the fridge and roll on a floured board to the desired size to fit the top of your pie. I always cut it with a 1" (2cm) overlap all around the edge to compensate for shrinkage. Before laying the pastry over the apples, brush the underside with egg to prevent the pastry from going soggy with the moisture from the apples. Once the crust is in place, cut a steam vent and brush over the remaining egg to give the crust a lovely golden colour. Cook for 20–30 minutes. Then take a quarter of the piecrust and present it separately from the apples, with perhaps some ice cream on the side. The rest of us enjoy our pie à la mode, as they say.

CHOCOLATE MOUSSE

A super-healthy friend from Los Angeles gave me this idea. This mousse is low in sugar and has a secret ingredient: avocado! With its high fat content, the avocado does the job of the heavy cream in a traditional recipe but with all the added nutritional benefits (according to the USDA[1]) of high vitamin K, B6, C and E, to name a few. I'll 'fess up to the avocado at some point!

ingredients

- 2 large ripe avocados
- 4oz (100g) chocolate (milk or dark depending on your preference)
- 2 tbsp honey (the set kind works best)

- 2 tbsp cocoa powder
- 3 tbsp almond milk
- 1 tsp vanilla essence

Method

Take the skin off the avocados and remove the pits. Also watch out for any fibrous tendrils and pull those out of the flesh and discard. Stringy bits in a mousse will definitely give the game away. Melt the chocolate in a bowl over a pan of barely simmering water. Then combine all the ingredients in a food processor until

---

1   See www.californiaavocado.com/usda-dietary-guidelines, accessed on 18 September 2014.

the mixture is smooth and creamy. Spoon the mousse into a large bowl or individual pots and place in the fridge for a minimum of an hour to set. Delicious!

DIY BUTTERFLY BUNS

These are a fun way to let your children create their own dessert and transform their plain cupcake into a pretty butterfly. With luck, they will happily take a bite of the cake and the cream cheese 'glue'. This recipe is also gluten-free.

ingredients

- 1½ sticks (150g) butter, softened
- ¾ cup (150g) superfine sugar
- 3 eggs
- 2 tbsp milk
- 2 or 3 drops of vanilla extract
- 1¼ cup (150g) brown rice flour
- 2 tsp gluten-free baking powder
- 5oz (150g) mild cream cheese
- 1 tbsp set honey
- Candied angelica to decorate

Method

Set out your bun tray with papers. I like to anchor mine with a tiny dot of butter so that when I spoon in the cake mixture, they stay put. This recipe makes 12–14 depending on how big you like your buns. Preheat the oven to 325°F/160°C/140°C fan/gas mark 3.

In a bowl, blend the butter and sugar with a wooden spoon. Then beat in the eggs, milk and vanilla, and fold in the flour and baking powder.

Put equal dollops of the mixture in each bun case. If you want the cooked bun to sit neatly inside its case, fill each case half full. But if you like a fuller protruding bun, then fill two-thirds up. Cook for 15–20 minutes on a middle shelf. Leave to cool on a wire rack. It's up to you, but I keep the paper cases on the buns as my children have always enjoyed peeling them off. When cool, take a sharp knife and cut a shallow cone out of the top and slice it in half. Then replace it in the bun. With a hand blender or a fork, mix together the cream cheese and honey. Present your child with a bun, the carved bits sitting in place, a ramekin of cream cheese icing and some angelica stalks that make great antennae. They will have great fun creating their very own butterfly by filling the cavity with the icing, placing the semi-circles on top to resemble wings, and adding the angelica 'antennae'.

Some like it tepid

I just wanted to address something that's key to serving food to my Asperger child and that's temperature. It seems that the temperature dial, as with the other senses, is cranked right up. Like most adults, I like to eat my hot food piping hot and my cold food, well, pretty icy. I have now finally figured out that my hot is Henry's scalding and my warm is Henry's hot, and that goes for the other end of the temperature chart too. Unfortunately, it took a very long time for this to register. I would put the dinner out, having made large efforts to produce exactly what I knew he would eat, only to be rebuffed. He would lean over and get his face close to the food and tell me he couldn't eat it. As we were all tucking in to our meals, upon my insistence he would take a bite and then scream and sob that it had burnt him. So meals were left to go cold and then only picked at suspiciously. Conversely, ice cream was thawed by Henry mushing it around until it formed a tepid soup. The temperature issue was really messing with my nerves because the object of this whole dietary exercise was to allow our family to sit down and eat a meal together. It wasn't working if one of us ate ten minutes after everyone else had left the table.

So, on top of the food choice and texture limitations, we now had another element to consider. Here's how I make it as painless as possible:

- Keep a stack of plates in the fridge! You might want to use Melamine or Pyrex as I don't think your best china would benefit from this regime. Ergo, Henry's plate cools the food faster and everyone at least gets to eat together!

- Put his food out ten minutes earlier than everyone else's.

- Give him a bigger plate so he can spread it out to cool.

- For ice cream and other cold food, warm a dish in the microwave for 30 seconds before serving. It is important, though, to make sure the plate isn't hot when you give it to him!

These tips and tricks will enable you to reclaim dinnertime for all the family. Start by choosing just one or two of the recipes that work best for you so that the ASD and neurotypicals all have something they can eat and enjoy. It's important. Sharing a meal is what binds us and keeps us whole.

Chapter 8

Eating Out

A Survival Guide

When mealtimes are challenging at home, why take this circus and lay it out for public display? That's pretty much what I ask myself when I am sitting in a restaurant with a twitching child who won't touch the food on his plate and is complaining that the lights hurt his head. But eating out is an important 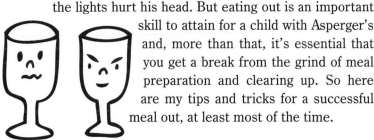 skill to attain for a child with Asperger's and, more than that, it's essential that you get a break from the grind of meal preparation and clearing up. So here are my tips and tricks for a successful meal out, at least most of the time.

Surveillance

As we all know, Aspergers hate surprises, but, armed with enough of the right information, I believe they can pretty much tackle anything. So build up to your eating event. Recce the place first yourself, check that it's suitable and then, in the lead-up to the meal, walk past it, drive past it and talk about it. Talk about it all the time: what food they serve, what you have seen on the menu that he'll like, that you spoke to the head waiter, Fred, and he seemed like a nice guy and so on. We 'normals', as Henry likes to call us, have a sophisticated tuning-out system, and there have been many times that Henry has said that he can't take a place because of the high-pitched whirr of the drinks freezer that I hadn't even registered. So don't ever be afraid to ask your child, 'How does this place feel for you?'

Now, you may think the next section on interiors is overdone, but light and colour and sound largely affect my child's ability to function. I feel it's really just an extension of getting to grips with how he connects with the food he puts in his mouth. This is a whole new world of exploration and stimuli that I was not aware of in the slightest until I started discussing it at length with my boy. Let's start with light. It's either light or dark, right? No! The best-quality light is daylight. It's a complex mix of wavelengths and colours and it's subtle. So perhaps your child will be more relaxed sitting by a window. We always seek out areas of natural light and, if at all possible, sit outside.

Eating in the evening means much less or no sunlight, of course, so choose your artificial lighting carefully. Harsh, gaudy-coloured or pulsating lighting is the absolute worst. On occasion, usually on a long car drive, where we have been forced to take a meal break at the kind of eatery with game machines that whizz loudly and blast out bright flashes of glaring light, it has been utter hell for my child. Mental torture. He could hardly breathe, let alone eat.

Remember that your child's sense dial is turned right up so that light and noise are amplified. For instance, what is apparently a normal level for piped music in most establishments is deafening to Henry, and the loud reverberating chatter – the kind that you get in museum and art gallery eateries – is utterly unbearable. Strangely, some of the interiors that children are supposed to like – bright colours everywhere, a super-saturated chroma assault – cause Henry the sort of mental anguish you'd expect from a horror film. We'd design our play area very differently.

So we like restaurants with a lot of windows or good-quality lighting (not bright, coloured, 'romantic' or dim) for the evening and a calm atmosphere; invariably, if we are forced to sit by a speaker, I will ask them to turn the music down. I am getting to be a bit of an audio campaigner, actually, because I don't know why we are forced to deal with nasty ambient music everywhere we go. Anyway, if they turn it down, that usually works. If they don't, we leave and I let the manager know the reason why.

Essentially, the restaurants we frequent have interiors that don't press those visual and audio stimuli buttons too hard. That doesn't mean to say they are as quiet as the grave and painted a muted green, although that sounds nice, doesn't it? One of our all-time favourite restaurants is a Nepalese eatery called Mount Everest in Evanston, Illinois, where we lived from Henry being two to nine and a half. It is rather a large space so even when it does get busy it never feels crowded. The décor is, I suppose, plain, with large Himalayan scenes painted on the wall. The tables have friendly burgundy under-cloths with white paper ones on top. Chairs are wooden, flooring is green and one wall is all windows.

The reason we especially love this place is because they do a buffet and buffets work really well for us. First of all, there's no waiting. We can get in there seated at a table and in two minutes the boys are up and away getting their food. I'll approach 'waiting in restaurants' and how to deal with it later, but not having to sit for half an hour for food to arrive is BIG. At age eight, Henry would come back with a plate of rice and maybe some chicken, and then proceed to devour the fabulous fresh-made naan breads that had been brought to the table. He would attempt to eat most of them and I would have to guard the basket, sending frequent glances back to the table when I went to get my food to make sure he wasn't sneaking any more.

You might think that a Nepalese restaurant with all the pungent smells and strong spicy food would be the last place on our list. But Henry loved this place so much that I think he accepted the highly seasoned fare and rich odours – maybe because the interior environment was so appealing. Plus, of course, he could still eat his bland food here. Mainly rice and breads, of course, but he did gradually work up to a very mild chicken tikka; if I scraped the skin off the legs, the meat underneath was succulent and nearly spice-free. I am also sure that regular exposure to this Nepalese food did help him explore stronger-tasting food later on. A desensitization process occurred whereby a weekly dose of curry smells and a tiny bit on his chicken helped him to develop a tolerance for it. At about age nine, Henry added to his core favourites of chicken, naan and rice: carrot and broccoli pakora, melon from the fruit salad, and even lamb and goat meat carefully scraped free of sauce. Incidentally, a child with hyposensitive food needs would also really love this type of restaurant for the intensity of the flavours and the calm ambiance.

This fabulous restaurant did have another key winning characteristic in that for every repeat visit to the buffet you were asked to take a fresh plate, and a waiter appeared from nowhere to whip the old one away as soon as you looked likely to leave your chair. This allowed Henry to go up and try a new food, on its own plate, every time. I tell you, the day he ate broccoli pakora, followed by chicken, interspersed with crammed mouthfuls of plain naan, I wept with joy.

The buffet gave Henry independence, and for me as a parent it afforded some quiet, desperately needed moments, Kingfisher beer in hand, to chat to my husband. This made for the most relaxing meal experience we had eating out as a family. Thank you, Mount Everest. We quickly became Sunday buffet devotees and got to be on first-name terms with most of the staff.

Surveillance checklist

- Recce the same time of day you'll be eating. A daytime visit is no good for an evening meal.

- How's the light? Natural or artificial? Bright, dim or flashing? Choose a naturally lit place for preference or mellow, even lighting with as natural a look as possible.

- Tune in to piped music and the location of speakers. Avoid noisy refrigerators and packed echoey interiors.

- Chat to the staff. Are they delightful and helpful?

- Check the menu has Asperger-friendly options. Will they leave sauces off steaks and glaze off the vegetables? Is the kitchen open to off-menu ordering? Better still, select a place that serves a buffet.

- Atmosphere, feng shui, zen, vibe, whatever: tune in to it. You know your child. Will they like it?

it is all about timing

We have our mealtimes evenly spaced to prevent sugar lows and bad moods. When booking a table, I always try to factor in the waiting, the ordering and more waiting time. If you eat lunch regularly at 1pm, you might want to arrive at the restaurant at 12.15. A hungry, twitching Asperger is fairly high on the challenging Richter scale and you don't want that. So plan to eat earlier than you usually do. One of my first questions when I call up to book a table is 'What time do you open?' Getting there in good time for lunch or dinner also pretty much guarantees you'll have the place to yourself, which is a joy.

Almost as good as a buffet are establishments that bring early starters. We have to be careful with this one and see that Henry doesn't binge out on crackers, taco chips or – his absolute favourite – fluffy bread rolls, and is then too full or carbed-out (too much processed carbohydrate makes him jittery) to eat a proper meal. So try to order an early protein starter. After years of munching bread and crackers to keep him occupied, we went through a cajoling and experimentation phase with starters and an unexpected success was deep fried calamari. This is a boy who won't eat a baked bean! I don't know why calamari works, but I also don't care. It arrives pronto and is great protein.

The eternal wait

Why is it that on the evening we choose to eat pizza at a particular restaurant, the stand-in chef is cooking and the waitress fancies the table of boys at the far end of the dining hall and is blind and deaf to our efforts to communicate? Service is always slower in a restaurant with an Asperger child, or maybe it just seems that way. Waiting for food to be served with a boy who is about to bounce off the walls is one of the most frustrating things I have had to endure. So here are some coping strategies:

1. Order ahead of time. Call the restaurant up, tell them you have a child who can't sit still and order from the online menu. I have had mixed responses to this. The American restaurants were most accommodating; perhaps they liked the fact we would be in and out more quickly. I can only really pre-order when my husband isn't joining us, as he thinks it's a step too far in our efforts to bend to Henry's needs. Actually, it is more about the fact that he just doesn't like to be managed this way and sees it as an infringement of his right to sit and mull over the menu. Which leads us to our next coping strategy.

2. Have a handbag stuffed full of books, tactile puzzles such as a Rubik's cube, origami paper, colouring pencils and lots of paper. Paper is heaven-sent. Play picture consequences, noughts and crosses (tic-tac-toe in the US) and hangman.

3. Failing all that, have a few verbal games up your sleeve. Our favourite, pinched and adapted from the children's TV programme Wild Kratts, is Creature Quiz and it has transformed our waiting times as Henry can happily keep it up for 45 minutes. (Beyond that I start screaming, but keep it all inside.) First, set the rules about what animals are being covered in the game. Only living ones? Land or water dwelling? Sometimes we go the whole nine yards and it's any animal that has ever existed, anywhere. These are usually really long games saved for restaurants that are on go-slow. Basically, someone has to think of an animal and, just like Twenty Questions, each person in turn asks a question with a yes or no answer. It helps to establish whether it's a vertebrate or invertebrate and then go through the animal classes: mammal, bird, reptile and so on.

4. Produce a surprise toy that needs to be constructed. Lego® make some great mini cars and monsters for all ages that

can totally absorb and relax your Asperger beyond your wildest dreams. Until, of course, they drop that key brick or connector thingy on the floor, and in a nanosecond you are down on your hands and knees under the table feeling about through goodness-knows-what while your child sobs that to lose this part will break the toy and end his world. And then you find it, wipe it and hand it over. And order is restored, or at least it is after another glass of the house's excellent Pinot Grigio.

The key is to stay relaxed and keep your Asperger focused on a book or a game while you wait. When Henry was small, one of us would wander around with him, looking out the window, finding where the bathrooms were and generally making up excuses to keep him up and about so he'd sit still when the food did actually arrive. But you can only do that for so long. Some eateries very smartly hand out puzzle pages and colouring sheets, but after Henry reached the age of about seven we had to start bringing our own entertainment. Many parents, not only ones with ASD kids, have their young children occupied at the table in one way or another. But increasingly the distraction of choice is electronic. I do really object to hand-held video devices, especially in a social setting, because you lose all contact as their brains are sucked into that nasty DS void. More than likely, the parents are on their smart phones texting or whatever too, doing just about anything other than talking to one another. My strategies for Henry allow him to focus sufficiently to be able to function in a new environment and the toys and activities are merely distractions to keep him sitting still. Games, pens, paper and everything else goes away the minute the food arrives. Although we have been known, on especially trying occasions, to keep a round of Creature Quiz going till dessert.

Of course, you will also begin to frequent places that are Asperger-child-friendly, keep the muzak turned low and indulge your child's particular proclivities with off-menu ordering. We love Pizarro, a tapas restaurant on Bermondsey High Street, because when I ask if they will make a three-egg plain omelette on a plate by itself, folded in half, the waiter doesn't bat an eyelid. And a large glass of Rioja for me, please!

Port out, starboard home

Contrary to what you might think, the upmarket, white-linen-table-clothed restaurants, quite apart from their devastating effect on the wallet, are some of the happiest places for us to eat. Primarily, I suspect, because they exude a calm, ordered atmosphere. There are rules of conduct and order to be observed, and this is very much welcomed in our world. Take a look at the place settings, for instance, with the formal layout for the cutlery, side plate and glasses. Actually, with so much going on there and sometimes with consecutive seating arrangements, it is difficult to keep track of what belongs to us. Here's a lovely child-friendly aide memoire for identifying which side is our bread plate and drinks glasses. Make a circle with the thumb and forefinger of both hands, keeping the other fingers straight. The left hand forms a 'b' for bread, the right a 'd' for drink. Social skills for life! In these houses of high etiquette, with starched linen napkins, if you order a steak it will quite often arrive on a huge white platter with vegetables served from a separate dish and the sauce on the side. Sufficient encouragement, I think, to get your Asperger to work hard at school and get a decent-paying job to allow him to frequent such high-class establishments, while treating his mother, of course.

Restaurant etiquette

From Henry being about seven, when we ate out, I made sure I gave him a quiet running commentary on what was happening. For example, 'This lady is going to show us to our table,' and, 'This is the drinks waiter, so think about what you would like to drink, and when he asks you, let him know.'

This gave Henry a mental map of where we were at in the proceedings and why, for instance, the drinks waiter was not interested in receiving his food order, and why the waiter wouldn't know we were ready to order until he could see we had put our menus down.

I am sure you get the idea. It is also important to instil some good eating-out manners into your child. Aspergers are unlikely to pick this sort of thing up by observing others, so it is helpful to lay the rules out clearly for them as you go through the meal. Here are a few of our rules. Use your own judgement about what age they can take on board this new information.

- Everyone takes their cue to start eating from the host putting their napkin on their knee. Daddy's paying, so we take our cue from him.

- Ladies should be served first in descending order of age. That'll be me!

- If you wish to refill your water glass, ask the person sitting next to you if they would like a refill before attending to your own needs. Ditto with second servings of food.

- When you get up from the table, place your napkin by your bread plate. Place it nicely, no need to fold it.

- When someone else gets up from the table, don't ask where they are going!

The list goes on. Eating away from home is also a good time to reiterate general good manners:

- Don't reach across the table; always ask politely for items to be passed to you.

- Sit up straight, keeping your elbows off the table.

- Never chew with your mouth open.

- Never talk with food in your mouth.

- Never put too much food in your mouth.

- Never mash or mix food on your plate.

- Do not blow on hot food or drink.

- Do not sip from a teaspoon.

- Never use your fingers to push food on to your spoon or fork.

- Don't rock back on your chair.

- Place your cutlery together on the plate when you have finished eating.

This is rather straightforward stuff and the rules are simple enough, even if, as in our house, they do need to be reinforced on a daily basis!

A more complex set of rules for an ASD kid are those subtle social edicts with several nuances, the interpretation of which depends entirely on the precise circumstances of the moment. Here's an example. I encourage Henry to meet people's eyes when at all possible. I know he can find this difficult, but if he manages it, eye contact makes a great deal of difference to the way he's perceived, particularly by people in positions of authority – teachers, for example. I have encouraged him to practise his eye-contact technique for a good number of years and now he really is very good at it. Then in a restaurant I have to explain why staring out the teenager on the opposite table is not done. 'Stop looking at him,' I say in one of those stage whispers that would shatter glass. 'Just stop, please. Yes, I know he's looking at you, but it's really not polite.' And there follows a convoluted explanation that has both of us more confused by the end of it.

Another classic, which no doubt you will be familiar with, is that as parents we encourage truth and honesty in our expression of what's around us and how we feel. But not when it involves Henry saying loudly, 'Why is that man eating so much when he's already very fat?' Or, 'That lady's just itched her bottom. That's rude, isn't it?' It is always a tricky one explaining why a rule we've been enforcing from day one doesn't actually apply in this situation. If we have run out of bread on our table, why can't we take some from the table next to ours? They are not eating it. It's a waste. Good luck to you with that one. I am sure, like us, you have a list of classic moments that invariably become amusing five years after the event.

when it all goes south and how to exit with your head held high

There are things you can do to cut down on mishaps when you are eating out and about. We always had a long-running history of knocked-over drinks. It got to the point where I almost expected to leave an eatery with wet trousers. Those to-go lids really don't cut it when a child hits a cup for six with a flailing arm. So we used to bring our own non-spill beakers. At first, when the boys were about two and three, we had the lidded 'sippy' cups with the spout and the valve that meant they had to actively suck to get the contents out. We soon gave those up, though, when I read the force of sucking was deforming kids' palates, and moved on to drinks bottles with the locked-down spout, which wasn't totally spill-proof, but if it did go over and you righted it fast enough, then only a small dribble would be lost. Then, when Henry was eight, I just couldn't stand the sight of those water bottles on the table any more and we made the rash move to real glasses; how else is he going to learn to respect the limitations of a water glass if he doesn't learn it now? And so followed many, many more wet trousers. I used to stockpile paper napkins by my plate in readiness. Even now, three years later, I spend the entire meal moving glasses about the table like chess pieces, out of range of disaster.

Other notable public displays in restaurants have included Henry dropping a plateful of food at a buffet: food and plate shards everywhere and in all directions, accompanied by a hysterical child, who was, bless him, trying to pick up the bits. But this sort of thing happens and usually everyone behaves in a way that makes the child know that accidents like this are really no problem. Occasionally, you will get a fuss-pot or a tutter, and my mantra to my children is always, 'Those that mind don't matter, those that matter don't mind.' And I think it is important to play the whole thing down, get him a new plate of food and, of course, grovel like crazy to the manager and tip heavily.

We've also had quite a lot of food spitting. You are no doubt familiar with this, when an unpleasant taste or unexpected texture has to be expelled immediately. To this day Henry will just spit everything out in the most revolting fashion, accompanied by crying, 'urhh' choking noises and a shuddering tick that shakes his whole body. Not an easy one to disguise in a busy restaurant and I have been known to throw a twenty on the table and make a discreet exit. Sometimes there's just nothing else to do.

But know that it's OK to be the parent with *that* child – that child causing the sensation that your fellow diners will relay later to wives, friends or work colleagues with pompous irritation or gleeful Schadenfreude: 'My god, there was this awful brat in the cafe spitting his food out all over the table. Nearly threw up my own lunch. The mother, useless cow, instead of dealing with him, kept going on about what it was that upset him. Needs a slap if you ask me. Of course, I complained to the manager...' Also know that there have been millions of good mothers like you, with the crying baby on the plane, with the toddler who crawled under the toilet stall door much to the surprise of its occupant! Someone's got to be that parent and today it's your turn. So suck it up, make your apologies, get the hell out of Dodge and know that in a couple of months, when your kid is bigger, they won't recognize you and it will be as if nothing ever happened.

Guest appearance

It is worth mentioning here that eating away from home doesn't always mean a restaurant, of course, but includes eating as guests at someone's house. 'Guest skills' are perhaps some of the toughest for an Asperger to manage because this is not a place where you order what you want, nor is it a place where you'll get things exactly how you like them. There are subtleties of behaviour here that are pretty tricky to grasp.

It is so nice to be asked over for food and I see my role as invitation acceptee as being to cause as little trouble as possible because I fully appreciate the effort the host is making to have us over. After inviting us, a host will usually ask, 'Is there anything you don't eat?' Well, now that's the sixty-four million dollar question, isn't it? My answer, you may be interested to know, is always, 'No. We eat just about anything.' Which is true, taken as a whole. Because the last thing I want to do is get into a long protracted discussion about Henry's dietary limitations, whatever they happen to be at that moment in time. If he had a nut allergy and anaphylactic shock was a consequence of my over-politeness, then fair enough, but over-sensitivity is just that and it can be managed. I know I wouldn't want to be told (in the nicest possible way) to tailor my menu choices for the meal to an individual's needs, because, quite frankly, I think that's rude. And I would rather, from a PR point of view, not make the meal about what my kid will or won't eat. To be fair, if they know you are bringing children, most hosts usually cook something that's not too adventurous. But if you pitch up, bottle of wine in hand, and they are serving Szechuan tofu with bang-bang shrimp and lemongrass, you have a problem and you may be forced to eat your words and quickly boil an egg.

Our rules as guests are

- It's not OK when the host hands you your meal to say, 'I don't like that. Do you have any plain chicken?' or 'What is it?' with a quizzical and disgusted look on your face. You will upset the cook. Instead, accept it graciously, trying not to grimace, and, if at all possible, eat *some* of it. Failing that, discreetly push it on to mine or your father's plate and we'll try to find you something else without making too much of a fuss about it.

- It is OK when the host is serving out the food to catch him or her early, either at the table or in the kitchen and say, 'No sauce/cream/gravy for me, thanks,' in preference to, 'Ugh! I can't eat *that!*' once it is out and in front of you.

- I explain that the host doesn't know your eating habits, likes or dislikes, and really it is not their job to know. This is good practice for dealing with unexpected options and it is important not to make too big a deal out of it.

- Most lunch or dinner parties have a selection of carbohydrate treats on offer and it is unfair to your child to expect them to avoid these tasty treats altogether. My strategy is to say to Henry that he must eat some protein – actually as much as he can manage – and then he may have a little of anything he fancies. Protein acts as a wonderful stabilizer and softens the behavioural effect of processed carbohydrates, especially sugar.

- Henry's weakness is bread and he can put it away at the most amazing rate. So we have words beforehand about how much bread he should consume. An instruction such as 'Don't eat too much' is counterintuitive because what's 'too much'? Too much is never enough, as far as Henry's concerned, so we use specifics: 'Eat two rolls, no more.' We can get into awful trouble if Henry has sunk the last of the fluffy white baps and asks the host sweetly, 'Any more bread?' When I chip in with 'He's fine, he's had enough,' it's as if I am talking about someone with a severe alcohol problem, throwing a 'don't push it' glance his way. The hostess invariably thinks I am just trying to save her the trouble and kindly heads off into the kitchen for extra supplies of bread rolls. More stern looks from me that may or may not go unheeded. Some whispering and bargaining invariably follows between me and the boy: 'If you eat more bread, then no dessert. Henry...'

- We both agree on a calm place where Henry can take time out from socializing, usually a quiet room where he can read.

With any luck, you will leave the party with genuine promises of reciprocation, and you and your child should both feel proud to have successfully navigated a challenging social and dietary event. It can only get easier!

Chapter 9

What Else Matters?

We have touched on how Henry's emotional state affects his approach to food. These are the signs to look for:

- fidgety and can't sit still

- repeating a movement or 'tick'

- whingy or upset

- refuses to come to the table or gives a long list of things he needs to do before he can eat

- zones out and is completely detached from what's happening around him.

So let's unpack that a little and think about what can be done so that an ASD child arrives at the table ready to eat with a calm body and a positive state of mind. Here are some of the elements that play into how well my Asperger eats.

For us, a key consideration is exercise

Without sufficient exercise Henry cannot sit still for two minutes; he can't settle his body, as he's all of a jitter. If he hasn't been running around expending energy for at least an hour in the morning, then he will not eat a decent lunch. School days are particularly difficult to manage. It seems that children nowadays are required to sit and sit and sit, virtually immovable for most of the day, with only a short morning break and very little midday playtime. My boys have attended schools where if it is so much as drizzling outside the children at lunchtime are given a film to watch, sitting again, to save messing up the school! Luckily, Henry attended a Steiner school in his early years where free movement was allowed. It was only after the age of eight, when he switched to a regular elementary school, that he had to comply with the sitting regime, which was absolute torture for him and messed with his emotional state.

To combat this, we made sure that we got some early morning exercise in – cycling, running to school, as much outside-time as we could – and tried to encourage the school to let him move about as much as possible by running errands for the teacher or doing a circuit of the gym when he'd finished his work. It is absolutely galling to have to explain patiently to a teacher why it is essential that a boy of eight gets regular movement breaks and that keeping him in at playtime, for whatever reason, is tantamount to cruelty.

The simple truth of the matter is that exercise calms the body and relaxes the mind, with the added benefit of working up a healthy appetite, and this is so much more important for a child with Asperger's. The children we know with Asperger's need masses of encouragement to get out and run around, particularly where there will be other children as these interactions can be disconcerting. The social challenges they face mean that they are much more comfortable by themselves buried in a book or a video game. Running around by yourself isn't much fun. So Henry and I came up with Asperger-centric exercise that can be done alone or with other kids, depending on how it's going that day.

- We love skipping. We bought a yellow men's fitness skipping rope so as not to be confused with the girly ones with the cute handles, and Henry keeps it in his school bag. At break times he skips. Sure, some of the kids make fun of him, but most of them want a go and now a number of children bring their own and they all skip rope together.

- We discussed the schoolyard jungle gym at great length and focused on parts of it that were separate and for the most part unused by the other children. Henry loved a hanging tyre and made it his go-to plaything, with the monkey bars as a back-up.

- Chalk in a tin in the pocket is very useful. Henry would make a starter mark, see how far he could jump from it, mark that line and then see if he could beat it. Other kids soon wanted to compete.

A game where virtually no effort has to be made, that attracts other children and is centred around a very definite activity is always a winner.

Exercise keeps things moving!

Exercise is also absolutely essential for digestion as it stimulates the contraction of intestinal muscles, which aids food absorption and helps move poos out of the body quickly and efficiently. As you all very well know, if you have been sedentary for any length of time, you don't feel like going to the loo quite as often as if you have been walking around. For a child with a diet that is already compromised and lacking sufficient fibre and water, shirking exercise has an even more dramatic effect on the intestine, and constipation can become a real issue. This further discourages activity. Who wants to run around with constipation? Who also wants to eat a good lunch when feeling all bunged up? It's all in a cycle and exercise goes a very long way to compensate and keep things moving along, even when a child's diet is less than perfect.

It is sensible, though, to wait half an hour to an hour after your child has eaten a large meal before sending them out to run around because they do need that initial quiet time when blood is directed to the stomach and intestines to maximize the effect of the digestive enzymes and nutrient absorption. So exercising too soon after eating directs blood flow to the heart and muscles instead of the digestive tract, and the food is left to make its way through the body only partially digested. As we all know, this leads to uncomfortable bloating and other well-known symptoms of indigestion! So the largest downside of incomplete digestion may be that your child associates eating with having an uncomfortable tummy afterwards, and this may hamper your efforts to get them to eat properly. Exercise is absolutely essential for children's healthy eating and digestion; just don't do it too soon after a meal!

Don't take a chill pill. Do this...

To eat well, I believe you must be calm and happy. If Henry's all hyper and outside exercise isn't an option, we do have a few other routes to a state of sangfroid.

Deep muscle tissue stimulation for relaxation

Like many Aspergers, Henry needs deep muscle stimulation to feel oriented and well. He finds intense pressure on his body incredibly calming. So since he was two, I have used several strategies to give him the pressure he needs. My first offer to him is always a strong, warm hug that can last two or three minutes, where I squeeze him all the way up and down his back – you can feel the tension in his body melt away. When Henry was very small and agitated, we would play our game called 'Seedling', where he would lie on the floor on his back, or sometimes squat and curl over, and I would cover him with heavy blankets, obviously making sure his head was in a position so he could breathe. Henry would lie there, loving the weight of the blankets on his body. After a few minutes, when he felt ready, he would shed the blankets and slowly grow upwards like a new shoot in spring, pushing his way through the frozen soil. And then he would grow leaves and buds and finally flower. And I had a happy, smiling boy again.

Walking up and down the stairs with a backpack filled with books also worked! Even now when we go on a hike, Henry asks to carry the backpack. Another great tip is to get your child to help with the heavy housework for pocket money or privileges or maybe, just maybe, because they *live* there! I happen to hate vacuuming and hauling round that great lumpen thing is an excellent de-stresser for Henry, so when he's vacuumed the whole house I am pathetically grateful and he's thoroughly relaxed. A beautiful symbiotic relationship!

Sometimes when Henry comes in from school or back from a play date where they have been sitting around, he's edgy and a little strung out, and I understand that if he doesn't dissipate that energy, it is going to wind him up until he snaps. I know him so well that I can see the tornado coming from a long way off. A cycle of uncontrolled and bad behaviour follows, and the obvious downside to this nervous state is that he won't eat, and if he does eat, he won't want anything that's good for him. We end up getting caught in a bit of a Catch-22. So at least an hour before mealtimes, if Henry is out of sorts, we do 10–15 minutes of what appears to be a military-style fitness regime and it is a very effective way of hitting all the major muscle groups. So we do maybe 20 press-ups, 20 star jumps, 10 burpees, 50 high knees, 50 sit-ups, running on the spot for a minute, and then we lie on the floor on our backs, relaxing with our arms out from our sides and our legs loose, all tension gone. If the military routine gets dull, switch it out for a boogie. Have some great music blasting from your iPod and shake a leg. Dance like you've never danced before (quite literally) and fling those arms and legs out, twist that torso and pogo like it's 1978. Better to choose a decent-sized space for this. Especially in the wintertime, we had late-afternoon basement discos that worked rather well. After half an hour of all that feel-good movement and letting go, I have a relaxed, happy boy ready to eat a good hearty meal and toned legs for my skinny jeans. Hurrah!

Water

Whether it is a lovely warm soaky bath or a pool, water has the most amazing mollifying effect on an agitated child. Henry has always had a special relationship with water: starting off with a water birth and being able to swim properly from the age of three. As a small child he had no fear of water, which gave me the absolute willies as he would jump into the deepest pools and sink right to the bottom, lying on the pool floor wearing an expression of absolute bliss. He later articulated that the weight of the water felt wonderful and what he wanted more than anything was an oxygen tank so he could spend an hour or two down there! All this aside, swimming and bathing are a wonderful pacifying tool that we use to balance the stresses and strains of everyday life, which in turn allows Henry to eat well.

Sibling friction

I am sure you know how disruptive sibling bickering can be. There has been many a time we have sat down to a meal with arguing children, and the upshot is always that Henry gets disproportionately distressed by the interactions and works himself into such a lather that he can't eat. His brother brushes off the angst and the insults and tucks into a pile of food, no problem. And this indifference further plays into Henry's anxiety, causing even more upset. Without a resolution, the snippy interchanges that dissolve Henry into hysterics can go on and on until either my husband or I, after many attempts to make the peace, send one boy or the other away from the table and the mealtime is ruined. Now I make it an absolute rule that arguments or even heated discussions are banned from the table. I won't have it. My digestion has to be considered along with everyone else's. We must have calm to eat well.

Alone time

We call it 'Henry time' and it is another important factor in maintaining a happy balanced Asperger child who feels comfortable and sufficiently confident to eat well. It is vital to respect their need to decompress, for the simple fact that there comes a point most days when they are maxed out with social interaction. I have seen mothers of ASD kids too painfully aware that their child shies from company push it on them over again, and it has the absolute opposite effect. Constant interfacing with others causes Aspergers great stress. I know that after a day at school Henry's nerves are strained to the limit and he must spend quiet time alone in a calm, safe space to recharge. Recharging, by the way, doesn't necessarily involve a screen; indeed, I prefer that it doesn't. Video games such as Minecraft are fantastic for Aspergers but they can overstimulate, so recharging for us involves a book, a puzzle or even origami, which is absolutely the best for destressing a pent-up child.

Be aware that inviting folks round to your house to eat can be massively challenging for your child. Understand that even if your guests are old family friends, this represents a significant intrusion, and if your child is required to sit and eat with everyone, don't make it the time you insist he finishes his green veg! If he sits for the duration of the meal and eats anything at all, he's doing really well. Be sensitive to the fact that your child needs to retreat from the hub-bub, so designate a quiet place, even if it is a cushion and a comic in the bottom of your closet, where he can be alone and regroup. Field any misplaced comments about his perceived antisocial behaviour or unfriendliness. Know your child and stand up for their needs. If you don't, who will?

Barometer

With his highly tuned senses and inability to shut off what affects him, Henry is our proverbial canary in a coalmine. He feels deeply and displays emotions that most of us should, if only we would pay attention to what is going on around us. We have had some rather large disruptions to our family life of late, notably the move back to Britain after a seven-year stint in America, a stressful and unsettling time for all of us. How I got through this transition was to put my head down and plough forward full-steam ahead, in an effort to get things done. My poor children must feel they are being bumped along in the wake. Although we do talk about what's going on, not everything is so well articulated, and some feelings the boys had about leaving the familiar and embracing the new surfaced in unexpected ways. Henry could always tell there was tension and upset, even if it was being suppressed. Henry feels the temperature of our family's emotional state and, since he has no screen, reacts immediately, and that's always the surest warning sign I have to slow down and take a closer look at how everyone's doing.

And so this brings me on to drawing your attention to your own state of calm. Be aware that what you say and do affects your child more deeply than you can ever realize. You may not see a reaction, but know that all your communications are being processed and are profoundly affecting. I battle with my own quick temper and sharp tongue because I know it hurts and scars. But we are all human, and if your temper does get the better of you, or a less-than-kind comment slips out, apologize and explain clearly what went wrong with that situation and how you are going to remedy your unfair actions. Above all, adopt a positive mindset towards your child, because you are affecting the way they navigate life and see the world. Your job is to give them the best tools to deal with life that ever you can.

Meditation

More recently, we have embraced meditation as a means to access a quiet and calm state when everything around us is challenging. This sounds super-hippy, I know, but it has been the most useful and effective tool when other calming strategies are unavailable. Practise with your child somewhere quiet and calm. We like our garden room, surrounded by the plants. Sit comfortably and balanced, on a firm chair with both feet planted on the floor, arms resting in a neutral position. Start by closing your eyes and focusing on the breath. We do eight slow breaths in and out, pause and then repeat, feeling the air going right into the body and then releasing it out into the world, maybe sending any bad feelings or unpleasant thoughts away with that breath. An extension of this is to practise clearing your mind of the noise that clutters it. We call it 'giving your head a holiday'. Sit still, your eyes closed, and push out all those unsettling thoughts, replacing them with a strong, calm image that makes you happy. I know some people like to imagine a ball of light that's warm and healing. Mine just happens to be a lake, a special lake for me. It's really a lovely conversation to have with your child, trying to figure out what that image will be. Or perhaps you decide that to be powerful the image has to be secret. Return to the breaths in and out with your own personal image filling your mind and take some beautiful, relaxing time out.

If you and your child practise this at home, you'll find that you can meditate anywhere and use it any time. Just for a brief second or two, take a step back from frustration or anger and replace those negative feelings with a beautiful sense of calm. And after a while you won't even need to close your eyes! Meditation is a reset button, a drug-free tranquilliser and, for a child with ASD, an absolute life-saver for controlling moods and outbursts.

Make happy

Henry frequently describes himself as feeling like an alien just beamed down from a far-off planet who spends his whole life trying to figure out what everyone means by what they say and what they do. He also says he gets told off from every angle because he's never doing the right thing. Quite apart from the fact that this makes me tone down the stream of instruction that I am apt to issue, it also gives me some idea of what he has to deal with minute by minute, every day. So, in the same way that meditation allows us to take a mental holiday, positive thoughts can achieve the same result, and this is one of the healthiest ways to change your child's mood or prevent them from being overtaken by negativity.

We all access good feelings and remember happy events, either consciously or unconsciously. Feel-good memories are powerful and a great stress-buster. But whereas we may do this automatically, I think children with Asperger's need to be taught how to recall happy times. It's just a way to think positively.

We have a mental checklist of happy things including (but not exclusively): our goofy miniature schnauzer's welcome and her attempts to lick your face and then roll on her back for a tummy rub; swimming at the beach; falling asleep in our garden room with its palms and fragrant flowers; FaceTiming old friends; the music from *The Voyage of the Dawn Treader* movie. Get your child to make their own very special and personal list and practise recalling that memory or event and excluding whatever else wants to barge into our mind space. Dear Reader, you know, of course, that I am no psychologist and I don't think this technique needs to be analyzed too deeply. But it is so simple and so important as an everyday defence for your child. These are tools that they can keep in their back pockets; just knowing they are there will make them feel a whole lot more confident.

Gate-keeper

I always tell my children that they are in charge of what goes into their brain. It is important to pay attention to this, because once a disturbing image or unpleasant event is in there, children with Asperger's are, I believe, more likely to dwell on it. Many real-life events are beyond your or their control, but what they see on TV or in a video game must be screened and is absolutely avoidable.

What are they watching or playing? Appreciate fully that violence or unpleasant behaviour strikes home with an Asperger child unlike anyone else. We don't allow any war games or emotionally charged TV or films. My boys are 10 and 11; they are just kids and I don't want them seeing that stuff. I am fairly horrified at what is deemed to be 'kid friendly' in other households and in society in general. But when they are on play dates I can't control what their friends' older siblings are watching or doing, so I say to my children that they have to be the guardians of what goes into their heads. Because once it is in there, you can't get it out.

Things you know but are maybe not doing enough

Does your Asperger know you love them? Tell them every day. Smile and hug your child to get that message through, because love fortifies like nothing else when they are out in the real world. Most importantly, listen. My child never says anything flippant or irrelevant, even though sometimes I may mistakenly take it that way. Make time for your child. And make time for yourself. It is tough parenting an ASD child. You are doing a good job and make sure you know it too.

Signing off

And so I hope this book sets you off in a better direction. Small life changes have reaped huge benefits for us and they can for you too. It all starts by seeing food through your child's eyes. This helps you work out a plan to introduce new foods. Upping the nutrient content of what they already like and desensitizing them to what they hate are all part of the programme. Day to day, it may seem slow going, but in two or three years' time, when you are all sitting down sharing a sumptuous lunch, you'll look back and know it was all worthwhile. Stay on track and the very best of luck to you.

Appendix

Food and Mood Diary

instruction

For each day of one week, fill out the form. Time and Place are easy. Pay special attention to your child's mood before they sit down to eat. Are they happy/sad/pensive/hyper/introspective/calm? And what is happening around them? Is it quiet or noisy? What distractions are there? Have they just been running around or sitting still? What's going on? Make a note of exactly what's eaten and any food they leave. Jot down snacks eaten: what and how much. If they are over-snacking, they won't be hungry for meals. Maybe they eat more varied foods at snack time; note that down too.

This information will give you a better idea of the quantity and quality of food your child consumes. It is something you can take to your doctors to get their perspective on your child's eating habits. You will see patterns of behaviour that correlate with eating well and eating badly, and this will help you set your child up for a much improved diet.

A template of this form is available to download from www.jkp.com/catalogue/book/9781849057684/resources.

★

MONDAY

	Breakfast	Lunch	Dinner
Time			
Place			
What else happening			
Child's mood			
What eaten			

	Morning	Afternoon	Evening
Snacks eaten			

★

TUESDAY

	Breakfast	Lunch	Dinner
Time			
Place			
What else happening			
Child's mood			
What eaten			

	Morning	Afternoon	Evening
Snacks eaten			

WEDNESDAY

	Breakfast	Lunch	Dinner
Time			
Place			
What else happening			
Child's mood			
What eaten			

	Morning	Afternoon	Evening
Snacks eaten			

★

THURSDAY

	Breakfast	Lunch	Dinner
Time			
Place			
What else happening			
Child's mood			
What eaten			

	Morning	Afternoon	Evening
Snacks eaten			

FRIDAY

	Breakfast	Lunch	Dinner
Time			
Place			
What else happening			
Child's mood			
What eaten			

	Morning	Afternoon	Evening
Snacks eaten			

★

SATURDAY

	Breakfast	Lunch	Dinner
Time			
Place			
What else happening			
Child's mood			
What eaten			

	Morning	Afternoon	Evening
Snacks eaten			

178

SUNDAY

	Breakfast	Lunch	Dinner
Time			
Place			
What else happening			
Child's mood			
What eaten			

	Morning	Afternoon	Evening
Snacks eaten			

Index

Index